The GHOST in the MIRROR

Karen Dolby

Illustrated by Brenda Haw

Designed by Kim Blundell and
Brian Robertson

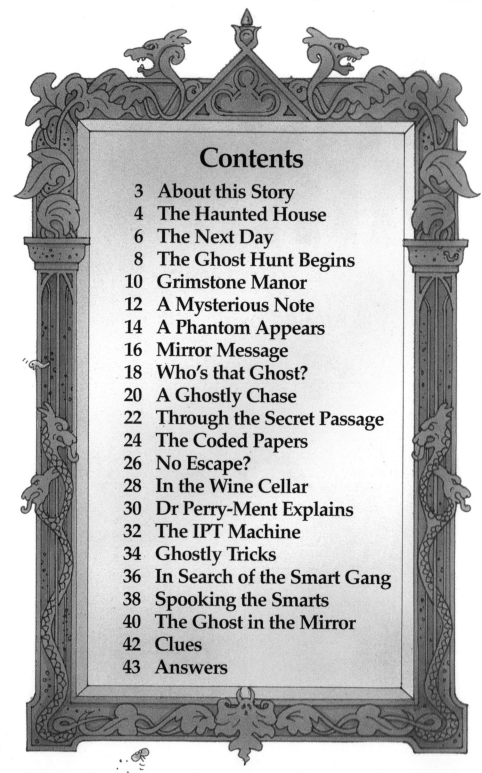

Contents

About this Story

The Ghost in the Mirror is a spooky adventure story that takes you on a ghost hunt through a creepy, deserted old manor house.

Along the way, there are lots of ghostly puzzles and perplexing problems to solve. Find the answers to these before going on to the next episode of the story.

Look at the pictures carefully and watch out for vital clues. Sometimes you will need to flick back through the story to help you find an answer. There are extra clues on page 42 and you can check your answers on pages 43 to 48.

Just turn the page to begin the adventure...

Sam, Joe and Polly were on their way home from school late one Friday evening. The gates to Grimstone Park were always locked, but this evening the gates are open. Should they go in? Sam leads the way...

GRIM STONE PARK

Polly

Joe

Sam

3

The Haunted House

Joe, Polly and Sam scuffed their way through the park, drawing closer and closer to Grimstone Manor. The house loomed dark and menacing above the trees.

"Here's the haunted house," Sam joked.

Joe peered through the gates. He had never been so close to the Manor before. Suddenly, an eerie green light glowed through one of the windows. Sam froze in horror as a flickering shadow appeared briefly at the window.

"There's probably someone living there now," Polly gulped.

"But the house has been empty for years," said Sam.

An owl hooted suddenly. Polly shivered. Grimstone Manor looked very mysterious. Sam's teeth chattered. He was convinced the house was haunted. But Joe was sure there was another explanation and wanted to investigate.

He stared up at the Manor. It was dark and creepy; the gates were locked; they didn't even have a torch. Perhaps it wasn't such a good idea.

"We'll come back first thing tomorrow," he said, finally.

The Next Day

Joe led the way back to Grimstone Manor, itching to begin the ghost hunt. Sam and Polly followed, struggling to keep up.

"Hide!" Joe whispered suddenly.

He pointed at two odd-looking people lounging against the wall ahead, talking in low voices. He didn't want anyone to see them sneaking around the house .

As they ducked behind some bushes, Sam tripped and dived head first through a small hole in the wall.

Polly and Joe crawled through after him and found themselves staring up at Grimstone Manor. In the daylight it looked empty and neglected and not at all scary. Joe marched up to one of the roughly boarded windows and tugged hard at a sheet of corrugated iron.

He quickly tried the others and groaned. They were securely nailed down and windows that had been left unboarded, were blocked by rubble. He stared at the house and in a flash, saw how they could get in.

Can you find a way in?

The Ghost Hunt Begins

Polly and Joe were soon inside. Sam had more trouble. Joe looped one end of the rope around the bannister rail and pulled. Sam grabbed the pole and Polly tried to haul him in. But Sam remained outside, dangling in midair. He was stuck between the two halves of the window and didn't dare look down.

At last they succeeded. Sam fell in and landed with a bump. He began to wonder if a ghost hunt was worth so much effort. But Joe was already thinking about where to start. It was a large, rambling house. How would they find their way around? The stairs going up were rotten and had collapsed, so they had no choice but to go down first.

Polly and Joe stared through the open door at a crumbling, cobwebby room which used to be a gift shop. The house had been open to the public once.

"It looks as if no one's been here for years," said Polly, venturing inside.

Suddenly she saw something that would be very helpful.

What has Polly spotted?

DINING-ROOM/GIFTSHOP

CRAFTS

LOCAL POTTERY

9

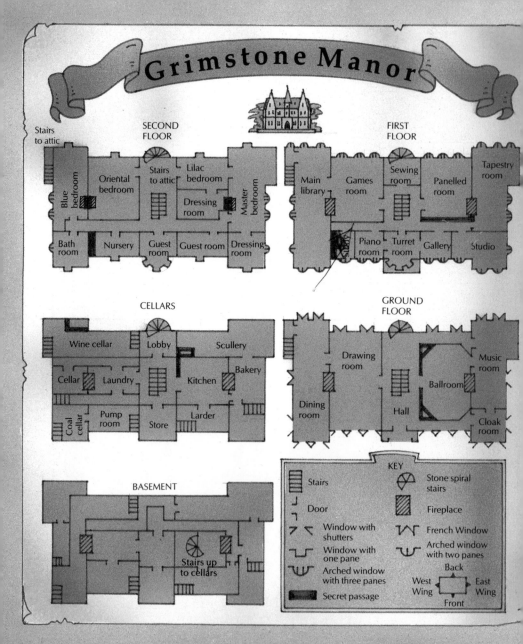

Grimstone Manor

SECOND FLOOR

Stairs to attic
Blue bedroom
Oriental bedroom
Stairs to attic
Lilac bedroom
Dressing room
Master bedroom
Bath room
Nursery
Guest room
Guest room
Dressing room

FIRST FLOOR

Main library
Games room
Sewing room
Panelled room
Tapestry room
Piano room
Turret room
Gallery
Studio

CELLARS

Wine cellar
Lobby
Scullery
Cellar
Laundry
Kitchen
Bakery
Coal cellar
Pump room
Store
Larder

GROUND FLOOR

Drawing room
Music room
Ballroom
Dining room
Hall
Cloak room

BASEMENT

Stairs up to cellars

KEY

Stairs	Stone spiral stairs
Door	Fireplace
Window with shutters	French Window
Window with one pane	Arched window with two panes
Arched window with three panes	Back
Secret passage	West Wing / East Wing / Front

S am read the short history of Grimstone Manor, shivering at the thought of strange lights, ghostly monks and secret passages.

He glanced around nervously expecting a ghastly spectre to appear at any minute.

"Where shall we go?" he asked.

10

Owners of Grimstone Manor

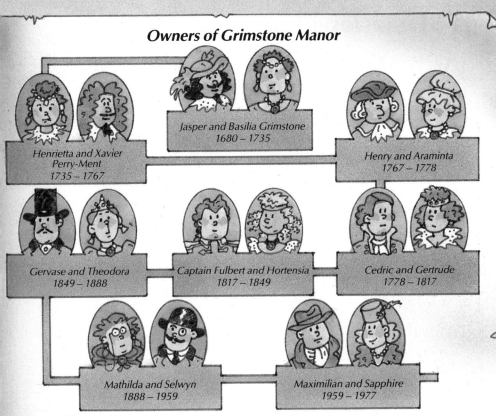

Jasper and Basilia Grimstone
1680 – 1735

Henrietta and Xavier Perry-Ment
1735 – 1767

Henry and Araminta
1767 – 1778

Gervase and Theodora
1849 – 1888

Captain Fulbert and Hortensia
1817 – 1849

Cedric and Gertrude
1778 – 1817

Mathilda and Selwyn
1888 – 1959

Maximilian and Sapphire
1959 – 1977

Grimstone Manor was built in 1680 by Jasper Grimstone. His only daughter, Henrietta, and her husband, Xavier Perrier-Mente, inherited the Manor in 1735. From that time, the house has been owned by the Perry-Ment family who have been known as the Counts and Countesses of Grimstone, since Captain Fulbert won the title for outstanding bravery. An inventive streak has always run through the Perry-Ments. While experimenting with gunpowder in 1862, Gervase blew up the East Wing and ballroom. These were later rebuilt by the brilliant architects, Sir John Truckbrugh and Sir Nicholas Hawksless.

The building itself is very mysterious. The thick walls hide secret passages and small rooms. There are also several secret and well-hidden doors with tricky, mechanical locks.

The Manor has more than its share of ghosts. It is supposed to be built on the site of a medieval priory and is said to be haunted by a spectral monk whose appearance is linked to strange, flashing lights. Visitors to the house have complained of sudden icy breezes, spooky noises and ghostly laughter.

"To the room with the flashing lights, of course," said Polly.

She studied the floor plans and thought back to last night.

She tried to picture the front of the house and soon knew exactly where they had to go.

Which room should they go to?

First Floor

11

A Mysterious Note

When they reached the study, the heavy door creaked open. Polly, Joe and Sam peered in uncertainly wondering what to expect.

"Someone's been in here," said Polly, pointing at the thick dust on the floor. "Ghosts don't leave footprints."

Feeling bolder, they began looking around. The room was disappointingly normal and there was no trace of anything ghostly.

It was hard to imagine the strange, glowing light and mysterious, shadowy figure they had seen from outside.

Sam picked up a curious-looking book lying on the armchair and flicked through. It was very old.

" 'Ancient Scientific Experiments that didn't Work'," he said, reading the title aloud.

As Joe glanced at the book, something else caught his eye.

Next to a dusty pile of books on the desk was a sheet of paper from a notebook. It was covered with writing and at first Joe thought it was written in a strange language. But as he looked more closely, he realized it was in code.

Can you decode the writing?

Rebmemer

ssap lliw uoy neht dna
elcric eht no sguj eht
ecalp ssalg a yb elttob a
ton elttob a no ssalg a
erom on teg lliw uoy
ro nwod thgir hsup
rood eht rof sserp dna
eniw eht rof sserp
reillem eht tuo ekat
dna selttob eht rof kool
rallec terces ym ot
krad eht morf og ot

A Phantom Appears

Even decoded, the note didn't make any sense. It was definitely human, but it just added to the mystery.

Joe looked up, gulped and grabbed Polly's arm.

"Look…" he gasped, turning a strange colour.

There, in the mirror was a terrible, ghostly apparition. Its face was shrouded, but Sam was sure it was staring at him.

"Let me out of here," he yelled, petrified.

A sudden, icy blast whistled through the room.

SLAM. Sam reached the door as it banged shut. There was a loud click and the latch dropped down on the other side, securely locking the door.

They were trapped in a haunted room. Polly stared into the mirror. The ghost had vanished, but who knew when it might return?

Sam hollered and tugged at the door, but it was no use. Joe rushed to the window. Feeling silly, he realized they were too high up to jump.

Meanwhile, Polly was thinking hard. There was something very peculiar about the large footprints on the dusty floor. They went in one direction only. The more she thought, the more sure she was.

"There's a secret door," she exclaimed, at last. "I know how we can get out."

Where is the secret door? Bookcase
How can they open it? Lever

Mirror Message

The bookcase swung open just like a normal door, revealing a flight of stone steps going up. They ran to a small landing at the top and Joe cautiously pulled the red lever in front of him. A panel halfway up the wall slid aside and they clambered out into an old nursery.

Polly rubbed her eyes. The wooden horse in the middle of the room was rocking to and fro.

"There must be a draught," she muttered.

Sam wasn't sure, but he thought the door opposite had just closed quietly. And weren't those footsteps fading into the distance? He jumped as laughter echoed around the house.

"It's the wind," said Joe, sensibly.

Just then, Sam shrieked and made a dash for the door. He had caught sight of a mirror. There was something in it…

"Come back," called Polly. "It's only writing."

Joe was already studying the mirror. He could see the outline of words written in the cobwebby dust, but they didn't seem to make any sense.

"It's another code," exclaimed Polly.

What is written on the mirror?

Who's that Ghost?

It was very puzzling. The note in the study and the mirror message were definitely NOT ghostly, but what about the figure in the mirror and the strange noises? And what about the creepy feeling they each had that they were being watched? As they stepped out into the corridor, the nursery door slammed shut behind them.

"I wonder what we'll find?" Polly said, nervously.

Almost before she finished speaking, she heard a low, wailing sound. It grew louder and louder, and closer and closer. Finally, a white, shrouded figure appeared, blocking the corridor ahead. It seemed to float towards them, howling horribly.

"It's the phantom!" Sam yelled.

Polly's knees turned to jelly, but Joe wasn't scared.

"You're no ghost," he shouted. "You don't frighten me."

Is Joe right? _yes_
What has he seen? _The back of the ghost in the mirror_

A Ghostly Chase

Joe dashed after the imposter with Polly and Sam hot on his heels. They skidded around a corner in time to see the ghost nipping into a doorway ahead. They ran into a large bedroom after him and stopped. Where was the ghost? Polly looked under the bed, while Joe checked a chest and Sam peered into an enormous wardrobe.

"Over here," he shouted. "It's a door to the next room."

The three climbed through the deep, empty wardrobe into a small bedroom. The white figure glanced back at them and made a hasty exit. Joe, Polly and Sam raced after him and saw the ghost trip over his sheet and fall downstairs.

They followed the ghost into a small room. This time he was trapped. There was nowhere to hide. Suddenly, they were plunged into darkness. Polly flicked on her pocket torch, but the ghost had vanished.

"How did he do that?" asked Sam. "We were blocking the door."

"There must be another secret door," said Polly. "But where?"

Polly thought hard. She was sure something was different. But what was it? If only she knew, it might give them a clue.

What is different?
Where is the secret door?

Through the Secret Passage

Polly had a hunch. She tugged at the silk bell pull, sure it would open the panel. They watched open-mouthed as the fireplace and part of the wall began turning slowly. Halfway round they saw the other, almost identical fireplace swinging into the room.

"Come on," Joe shouted, jumping onto the grate.

The fireplace jolted to a stop in a wide passage. Joe briskly led the way forward. Polly held the torch.

There were strange scuttling noises, loud dripping and their footsteps echoed loudly. Every sound was magnified and it was also very dark. Their torch beam barely pierced the blackness as they crept gingerly down a flight of slippery, stone steps.

"I don't like this," groaned Sam, fighting his way through a cobweb with a rat scuttling across one foot.

Polly had to admit she was feeling a bit spooked and even Joe jumped when he came face to face with a glowing skull leering horribly at him. Finally, they stumbled down a second flight of steps into a narrow bedroom.

There was no sign of the ghost, but there were two small pinpoints of light halfway up the wall. Joe took the first turn to look through the spyholes and peered into a kitchen. He gulped, scarcely believing his eyes.

In a dusty, mirror, he saw the ghostly figure from the study. It seemed to stare through him. He could have been mistaken, but before it faded away, Joe was sure it made a sign as if warning him to be quiet.

The Boss will be pleased with the plan we've stolen.

Mmm… But we've still got to find the Doc and his secret laboratory, Rex.

Immediately, two people walked into the kitchen and Sam replaced Joe. He frowned as he heard snippets of their conversation. What were they up to?

We've seen that girl before," Polly gasped, taking her turn at the spyholes. "But where?"

Where have they seen the girl?

23

The Coded Papers

As soon as the sinister duo had gone, Sam yanked an old white lever high up in a beam. There was a loud CLICK. A panel sprang open and promptly shut as they climbed through.

"Look," said Polly, running into the room. "They've left this behind."

An official-looking file was lying on the table. Feeling a bit guilty, and making sure they really were alone, they quickly opened it.

Inside, there were two typed sheets, masses of photographs of the same person and a yellow, blue-print plan.

"This might tell us what's going on," said Joe, "... if only we could read it."

Most of the writing was in an impossible-looking code. Polly scratched her head and studied the words. Perhaps it wasn't so tricky after all.

Can you decode the writing?

No Escape?

Sam, Joe and Polly flicked through the rest of the papers and photos.

"This must be Dr X. Perry-Ment," said Joe, holding up one of the prints.

"And this is a plan of part of his invention," Sam added. "I wonder what it does?"

More importantly, WHO was Dr X. Perry-Ment and why was the Smart Gang looking for him?

"It's up to us to find some answers," said Joe. "I'm sure that creepy duo are up to no good. There's something fishy going on."

But there was no time to sit and wonder what.

Polly heard voices growing louder. The Smarts were returning! Sam and Joe fumbled frantically with papers and photos, desperately trying to cram them back into the file. Polly began looking for a way out.

Joe ran to the secret door. But there was no lever to open it from this side.

Polly opened the door from the bakery, only to find the steps were rotten.

Sam tugged frantically at the larder door but it was locked and wouldn't budge.

Polly thought of the scullery but there was nowhere to hide or escape to in there. Just in time, they dived for cover in the only place they could see to hide. Heavy footsteps stomped into the room.

Silently, Joe pulled out the guidebook and map. There MUST be another way out... and they had to find it, fast.

Can you find another way out of the kitchen?

In the Wine Cellar

While the duo searched the bakery, Joe heaved open the trapdoor. They jumped down onto the flight of stone steps below and Sam shut the door before the crooks returned.

They ran through a maze of dark passages until they reached the large wine cellar below the dining room. A strange green glow shone through what seemed to be a solid wall. It reminded Joe of the flashes they had seen the night before. The glow traced the outline of a door. Could it be another secret entrance and the way in to the Doctor's laboratory? Joe tapped the wall lightly.

Sam wondered if it was such a good idea to try to get in. But if the creepy Smart Gang were after the Doctor, surely they should be on his side. Meanwhile, Polly stared at what Sam was standing on and gazed around the cellar.

"An electrical circuit," she exclaimed, with a flash of inspiration. "Where's the note we found in the study? It tells us how to open the door."

Can you work out how to open the door?

Wine · good year
709 BC   1474
404 BC   1989
1066   1989
1371
1525
465

Dr Perry-Ment Explains

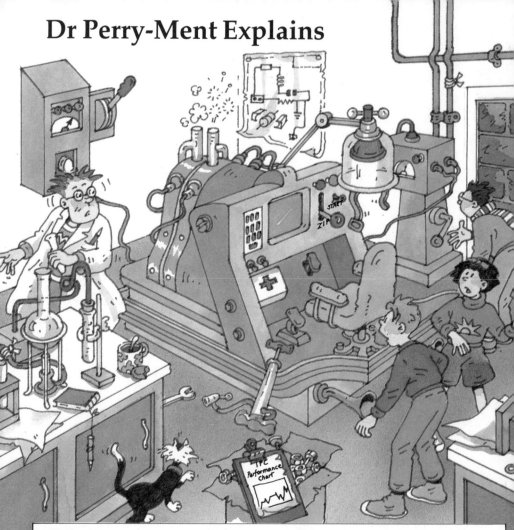

There was a loud whirring sound and several clicks. The door slowly opened and they stepped through into a laboratory. At first, no one noticed the eccentric figure half hidden by a peculiar machine. But he had seen them.

"I know who you are," he said, looking alarmed. "You're working for the Smart Gang."

Polly tried to explain, but Dr Perry-Ment was still suspicious. If only they could prove they were nothing to do with the Gang. Suddenly Sam remembered. He did have something which belonged to the Doctor. If he gave it back, Perry-Ment would know they weren't working for the Smarts.

What has Sam got?

"Now I know you're on my side you can help me to spook the Smarts away," the Doctor said.

Joe, Polly and Sam looked a bit puzzled as the Doctor began to explain.

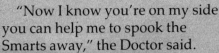

I am a scientist and I was working on a top-secret project when I made an amazing discovery…

I inherited the Manor 12 years ago, just as my granny had told me when I was a small boy.

… an incredible invention. But one of the junior scientists was working for the evil Smart Gang and they plotted to steal it.

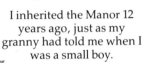

What could I do alone? A bodyguard will be here tomorrow, but in the meantime I decided to frighten the Gang by dressing up as a ghost. Now you're here it will be much easier.

The Manor seemed a perfect hiding place. I moved in and set up my laboratory here. My invention is a machine that moves people from place to place, instantly.

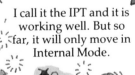

I call it the IPT and it is working well. But so far, it will only move in Internal Mode.

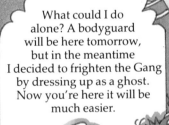

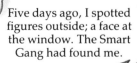

Five days ago, I spotted figures outside; a face at the window. The Smart Gang had found me.

The IPT Machine

Polly and Joe looked doubtful. The Doctor's plan sounded crazy. But it was their only chance to outsmart the Smarts and help Perry-Ment. First, they would need some ghost outfits.

"The Gang are searching the house again. We'll surprise them in the Games Room," the Doctor said, hurrying off to the attic with Polly. "See you there."

Polly dug out an old white dress from the dressing-up box. She pulled it on and covered herself with smelly white powder.

Sam tried on the Doctor's ghost outfit. He had to make a few alterations to make it fit, but he thought he looked very spooky in the end. The first aid box gave Joe an idea. It took him ages to unwind all the bandages and wind them around himself, but he decided it would make a brilliant fancy dress.

At last they were ready. It was then that they realized they were trapped. The only door was the secret one they had come in by and neither could see how to open it from this side.

"I know," exclaimed Sam. "We'll use the machine."

But how did it work? Sam pulled the START lever. Instructions flashed onto the screen. He had seen the ZIP stick but what was the ZAP number? There weren't any numbers on the machine. Suddenly he gasped. In the screen he could see a face… the ghost! He watched in horror as it's arm reached out towards him.

But the ghost was trying to help them. It pointed at a book which was the IPT handbook. As they began to read, they realized they could work out the ZAP number and which keys to press on the machine.

What is the ZAP number? Which keys should they press?

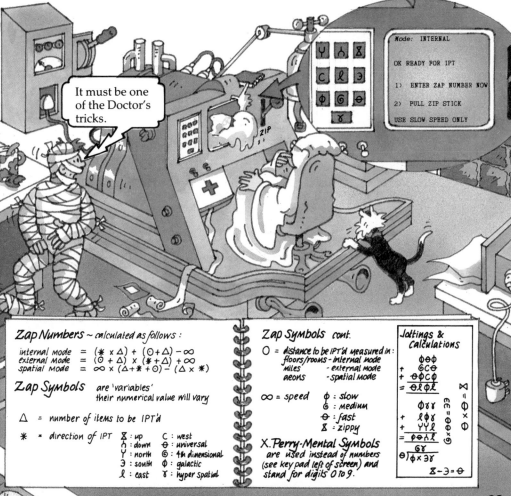

It must be one of the Doctor's tricks.

Mode: INTERNAL

OK READY FOR IPT

1) ENTER ZAP NUMBER NOW

2) PULL ZIP STICK

USE SLOW SPEED ONLY

Zap Numbers ~ calculated as follows :

internal mode $= (* \times \triangle) + (\odot + \triangle) - \infty$
external mode $= (\odot + \triangle) \times (* + \triangle) + \infty$
spatial mode $= \infty \times (\triangle + * + \odot) - (\triangle \times *)$

Zap Symbols are 'variables' their numerical value will vary

$\triangle$ = number of items to be IPT'd

$*$ = direction of IPT
    ਠ : up   C : west
    ਨ : down   θ : universal
    Ψ : north   Θ : 4th dimensional
    Ꙩ : south   Φ : galactic
    ℓ : east   ɣ : hyper spatial

Zap Symbols cont.

$\odot$ = distance to be IPT'd measured in:
    floors/rooms - internal mode
    miles - external mode
    aeons - spatial mode

∞ = speed   φ : slow
                6 : medium
                θ : fast
                ɣ : zippy

X.Perry-Mental Symbols are used instead of numbers (see key pad left of screen) and stand for digits 0 to 9.

Jottings & Calculations

$\phi\theta\phi$
$+ \quad 6C\theta$
$+ \quad \theta\phi C\phi$
$= \overline{\theta\ell\phi\ell}$

$\phi\delta\gamma$
$+ \quad \ell\phi\gamma$
$+ \quad YY\ell$
$= \overline{\phi\theta\wedge\ell}$

$\theta\ell\phi \times \exists\gamma$
$\dfrac{6\gamma}{\quad}$

$(\gamma\times\theta\theta = \exists\exists)$

$\exists\times\phi = \wedge$
$\phi\times\phi =$

$\gamma - \exists = \theta$

Ghostly Tricks

The machine whirred, buzzed and rattled. It finally shuddered to a stop in a cloud of green smoke. Sam blinked. With a start he realized they were in the library. Joe tapped in the ZAP number and sent the machine back to the laboratory.

Polly and Perry-Ment were hard at work in the games room. The Doctor was brushing florescent paint onto plastic skulls which made them glow eerily in the gloom and Polly was trying out a trick she had read about with dried peas, a glass and a metal tray.

Sam had an idea. He and Polly could be a headless ghost. He found her a black hood and then dashed behind a black curtain. As he balanced on a stool with his head tucked under Polly's arm, he tried to ask the Doctor about the ghostly figure.

My uncle used to put on magic shows here so there are lots of props.

The peas at the bottom swell and push out the ones on top. So they rattle down onto the tray and make a spooky noise.

But the Doctor was busy. He had decided to try an old trick from his uncle's book using a special chair and a mirror. His head was supposed to look as if it was floating in midair. But although he read and reread the instructions, he couldn't make it work. Finally he gave up.

Meanwhile, Polly and Sam had discovered a large mirror at the back of the stage with a lever to tilt it.

"Pepper's Ghost," exclaimed the Doctor. "That's one trick that will work."

He told Joe to jump into the pit and stand below the floodlight where he couldn't be seen. Sam was to carry on tilting the top of the mirror down towards the stage.

What will the audience see?

35

In Search of the Smart Gang

They ran to their ghostly positions as footsteps grew louder and closer. There were voices in the library, but they faded away as the steps carried on downstairs.

"There's someone in the hall," hissed Sam. "They're coming this way."

They came closer and closer... but no. They too carried on past.

"We'll just have to go after them," exclaimed Dr X. Perry-Ment.

Joe and the Doctor hurried into the library while Polly and Sam ran into the hall.

They tiptoed around the rest of the floor, peering cautiously into each room, but they found no one. Suddenly a board creaked behind them. Polly froze, then sighed with relief when she looked back. It was only the cat.

"Let's look downstairs," she said, feeling braver.

They crept down and stopped. Voices coming from the drawing room! This was scary.

What were they supposed to do now? Sam gulped and turned the handle slowly. There was silence on the other side of the door.

"Come on," Polly croaked.

They flung open the door and leapt into the room, trying to look as frightening as possible. BANG, CRASH, THUD. They collided with two other, very solid ghosts... Joe and the Doctor.

"This is useless," said Joe, picking himself up.

"We'll never scare the Gang like this," he added.

"Wait a minute," exclaimed Polly. "What's the time? I think I know where we can find all four Gang members together."

Where will they find the Gang?

Spooking the Smarts

The Doctor led the way to an incredible octagonal ballroom which was lined from floor to ceiling with mirrors. He held up his hand in front of one of the panels. It slid open and they stepped into a small, secret room, where they could hide and wait for the Gang. The walls were one-way windows and they could watch the ballroom. Although it was impossible to see into the room from outside.

The last to arrive was a sinister-looking girl wearing dark glasses. She seemed to be the boss.

"Well?" she snapped at the other three who looked very sheepish. "Have you found anything yet?"

Now was their chance. The Doctor released the panel. The four "ghosts" leapt out and the panel slid silently shut.

The Gang looked surprised, but not a bit frightened. Then suddenly the spy called Rex gasped. Seconds later, all four Gang members took to their heels. Looks of utter terror were on their faces.

Why? Joe and Polly were puzzled. Then Joe caught sight of something. Now he understood.

What frightened the Gang?

The Ghost in the Mirror

The ghost chased after the Gang, hovering in midair, howling. Joe, Polly, Sam and Perry-Ment raced after them. They reached the hall in time to see Rex cowering, petrified, by the front door.

He was desperately trying to open it. But at last he gave up and ran after the rest of the Smarts. With the ghost in hot pursuit, the Gang dashed along the corridor and straight on through the drawing room.

"Let me out of here!" yelled Rex, running into the dining room.

Joe and Polly watched from the door as the Smarts fumbled with one of the barred windows. The boss was already halfway through.

Seconds later, the last of the Gang clambered out. Polly, Sam and Joe ran into the room and watched incredulously as the ghost melted back into the mirror. Sam was sure the phantom smiled as it began to fade away.

"That's got rid of them," exclaimed Joe, watching the creepy quartet race away.

Sam stared at the mirror where the ghost had vanished. There was one final question.

Who was the ghost in the mirror? The Doctor smiled mysteriously. It was someone he knew very well. Polly thought she knew the answer.

Who is the ghost in the mirror?

Clues

Pages 6-7
Is there an open window? They can use the rope and hook.

Pages 8-9
Look for something to help them find their way around the house.

Pages 10-11
The window with the green light is on the first floor.

Pages 12-13
Think backwards.

Pages 14-15
Where do the footprints lead? Look at the book titles on page 12.

Pages 16-17
Try exchanging the last letter of the first word with the first letter of the second word.

Pages 18-19
This is easy. Use your eyes.

Pages 20-21
Use your eyes again.

Pages 22-23
Flick back through the book.

Pages 24-25
A different code is used on each document. Extra letters have been added to one.

Pages 26-27
Look at the map again. Where are they? Can you spot a hidden door?

Pages 28-29
Look at the note on page 13.

Pages 30-31
Has Sam picked anything up recently?

Pages 32-33
Hint:
Number of persons = 2
Direction = 9 (up)
Distance in floors = 2 (cellars to first floor)
Speed = 1 (slow)

Work out which X. Perry-Mental symbols stand for which numbers by solving the sums in the handbook.

Pages 34-35
Think hard and use your imagination.

Pages 36-37
Look at the mirror message on page 17. What is the time?

Pages 38-39
Look carefully at everyone in the ballroom and their reflections.

Pages 40-41
Look at the paintings and the family tree on page 11.

Answers

Pages 6-7

Using the pole with the hook, they pull down both ends of the rope pulley. The rope is hooked around the tyre and Joe sits in it, holding the pole. Polly and Sam hoist him up until he is level with the open window. He then hooks the pole on the window bar and swings himself inside. The tyre is lowered and Polly is hoisted up by Sam. Joe holds out the pole and drags her in. He then pulls in the free end of the rope using the pole. Polly and Joe lower the tyre again and then haul Sam up, again using the pole to drag him inside.

Tyre Pole with hook Rope pulley Open window

Pages 8-9

Polly has spotted a guide and map to Grimstone Manor.

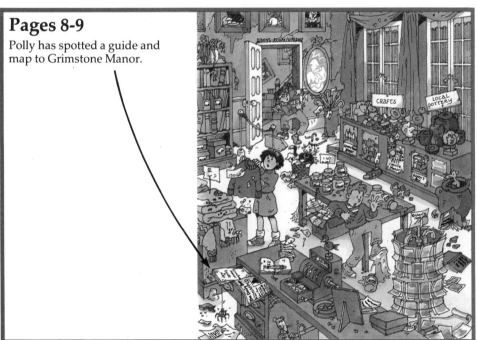

43

Pages 10-11

They should go to the study on the first floor which was where the strange glow came from on the previous night.

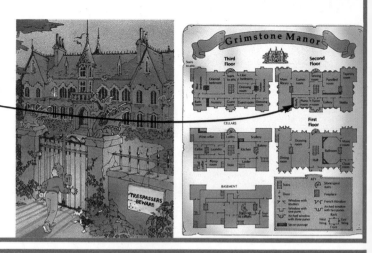

Pages 12-13

The note is written backwards. This is what it says with punctuation added:

To go from the dark to my secret cellar, look for the bottles and take out the Mellier. Press for the wine and press for the door, push right down or you will get no more. A glass on a bottle not a bottle by a glass. Place the jugs on the circle and then you will pass.

Remember

Pages 14-15

The footsteps go towards the bookcase which is the secret door. The handle is the book called HANDEL by I.M.A Lever.

Hidden lever

Footprints

Pages 16-17

The message is decoded by swapping the last letter of each word with the first letter of the next. It says:

Search everywhere. The lab must be found. The machine will be mine. Meeting 15:30 hours, ballroom. The Boss. Code X

Pages 18-19

Joe is right. He has spotted the rear view of the ghost in the mirror, which clearly shows someone wearing a ghost costume.

Pages 20-21

The fireplace has changed which suggests it is a secret, revolving door and that there are two fireplaces.

The differences are ringed here.

Pages 22-23

They saw the girl standing outside Grimstone Manor on page 6.

Pages 24-25

The first document has one extra letter (or number) added in front of each group of letters. It is decoded by taking away the first dud letter and then amending the spacing to make words. It says:

THE SMART GANG DOSSIER 1
FACTS KNOWN
Name: Dr Xavier Perry-Ment
Born: 4 December 1950

Moved into Grimstone Manor in early September. Under Smart Gang surveillance since 10 September. World famous scientist working on top secret invention – Instant Physical Transference machine. Uses his own special code to work the machine in which symbols equal digits 0-9. Smarts still working to break code. He also sometimes uses a word code for his notes.

Code K

Pages 24-25 (continued)

The second document is decoded by swapping the first and last letters of each word. It says:

SMART GANG DOSSIER 2

Gang's uses for the machine:

could be rented to other crooks; entry to bank vaults, museums and galleries (and quick exits with loot leaving no trace); entry to government offices.

Operation Perry-Ment commences 12:00 hours on Saturday 24 September.

Code T

Pages 26-27

The map on page 10 shows a stone spiral staircase leading from the basement up to the cellars. This is in the room directly below the kitchen. You can see the hinges and edge of a trapdoor hidden below the rug where Polly, Joe and Sam are hiding.

Trapdoor

Pages 28-29

The door is opened by completing an electrical circuit. Polly works out how to do this from the coded note they found in the study on page 13.

They have to:

1) Remove the wine bottle labelled Mellier;
2) Press the wine press down;
3) Find the bottle with a glass on the label and take away the bottle and glass next to it;
4) Place the eight jugs on the dark stone slabs. (There are contact points on the slabs and also on the bottom of the jugs.) Sam is standing on the battery which powers the circuit.

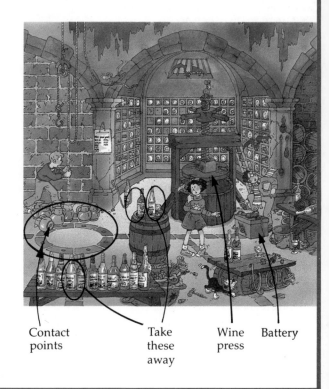

Contact points

Take these away

Wine press

Battery

Pages 30-31

Sam has Dr Perry-Ment's plan of the IPT motor. When the Smarts were returning on page 26, he crammed the yellow plan into his pocket without thinking. It is still in his pocket on page 29 in the wine cellar.

Page 26

Page 29

The plan

Pages 32-33

There are ten X. Perry-Mental Symbols and each one stands for a different number from 0-9. You can decode all the symbols by working out the Doctor's simple sums scribbled in the margin of the handbook.

X. Perry-Mental Symbols:

ၓ	φ	၆	ꝋ	C	ℓ	Ꝫ	Ψ	ᓂ	Ҳ
0	1	2	3	4	5	6	7	8	9

The handbook shows the formulae for three Zap Numbers. The correct formula depends on the machine's Mode. The screen display shows the machine is operating in Internal Mode and says to use Slow Speed only.

The symbols used in the formula are explained in the list of Zap Symbols. The numbers they represent vary, but for Joe and Sam's move they are as follows:

Numerical value of each variable Zap Symbol:		X. Perry-Mental Symbols
number of people	= 2 (Joe and Sam)	၆
direction	= 9 (up)	Ҳ
distance in floors	= 2 (cellar to first floor)	၆
speed	= 1 (slow)	φ

So the equation to find the Zap Number is:
$$(9 \times 2) + (2 \times 2) - 1 = 21$$

The Zap Number is 21 and in X. Perry-Mental Symbols this is ၆φ. These are the keys which Sam must press.

Pages 34-35

Pepper's Ghost is a famous trick. If Joe stands down in the pit so he can't be seen and the mirror is tilted, his image will be projected up onto the stage. The audience then see a ghostly image appear.

The diagram shows how Pepper's Ghost works.

Pages 36-37

They will find the Gang in the ballroom at 3:30 p.m. (15:30 hours).

The mirror message on page 17 is from The Boss, the leader of the Smart Gang and it arranges the meeting. Dr Perry-Ment's watch shows the time is now 3:20 p.m. They still have time to reach the ballroom before the Gang members arrive.

Pages 38-39

Polly, Joe, Sam and the Doctor are all reflected in the mirrors, but there is one extra ghostly figure who has no reflection. This must be a real ghost.

The real ghost

Pages 40-41

The ghost is Mathilda, the Doctor's grandmother. Her portrait is in the family tree on page 11 and there is also a painting of her in the dining room. When you first see the portrait, Mathilda is frowning, but in the final picture her portrait is smiling after frightening away the Gang.

The ghost

The portraits . . . before and after

Mathilda

Before

After

DANGER AT DEMON'S COVE

Karen Dolby

Illustrated by Graham Round

Designed by Graham Round and Brian Robertson

Contents

About this Story

Danger at Demon's Cove is an exciting adventure that takes you on an ancient trail in search of the amazing Demon's Eye Diamond and lost treasure.

Along the way, there are lots of tricky puzzles and perplexing problems which you must solve in order to understand the next part of the story.

Look at the pictures carefully and watch out for vital clues and information. Sometimes you will need to flick back through the story to help you find an answer. There are extra clues on page 89 and you can check the answers on pages 90 to 96.

Just turn the page to begin the adventure...

Sally

Max

Max and Sally are on holiday. They are camping outside their grandparents' house on the cliff top above Demon's Cove. Between them, they manage to find all the clues and solve the mystery. Can you?

51

A Dark and Stormy Night

It was a dark and stormy night, long ago. A ship called the Indian Queen was on her way home from the East, loaded with spices and silk. There was also a secret cargo belonging to a fabulously rich prince which Captain T. Clipper had pledged to guard with his life – an amazing hoard of treasure, including the Demon's Eye, a huge, priceless, black diamond.

The Indian Queen was lashed by fierce waves. The Captain struggled to steer the ship and desperately looked out for the lighthouse beam.

Meanwhile, the three evil Grabbitt brothers waited on the cliffs above Demon's Cove, sending a false signal to lure the ship onto the rocks.

The Captain spotted the signal. The doomed Indian Queen unwittingly sailed onto the treacherous rocks and began sinking fast.

Denzil, Jago and Joshua Grabbitt eagerly hauled the cargo onto the shore, without a thought for the crew of the wrecked ship.

The Indian Queen sank without trace, while the brothers inspected their booty. Denzil, the most evil of them, prised open the chests.

The greedy Grabbitts stared incredulously at the glittering jewels and amazing treasure, hardly able to believe their luck at such a haul.

Tom paused and gazed out to sea. Sally shivered. She could picture it all clearly.

"But what happened to the treasure?" asked Max. "What did the Grabbitts do with it?"

"It's said that they hid the two treasure chests in the maze of smugglers' tunnels at Demon's Cove," Tom continued. "But within months the brothers had mysteriously perished and the secret of the treasure was lost with them.

Some say the Demon's Eye diamond held a curse. No one knows for sure. But even now, ghostly cries are heard echoing through the caves and on stormy nights the phantom Indian Queen can be seen sailing in the bay at Demon's Cove."

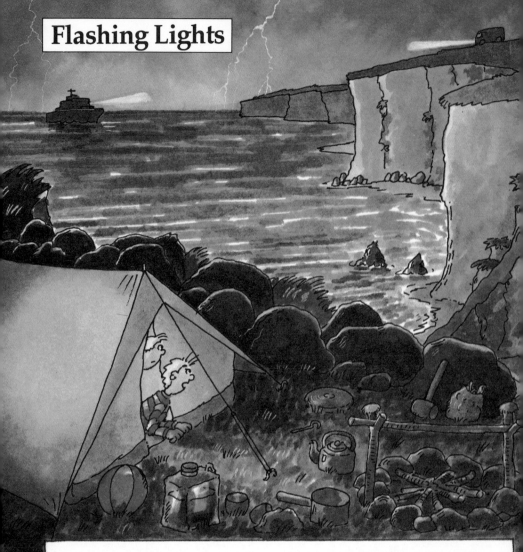

Flashing Lights

Later that night, Max and Sally were asleep in their tent on the cliffs above Demon's Cove. A sudden loud roar of thunder woke Sally with a start.

She peered out through the tent flap as lightning lit up the bay. Sally rubbed her eyes in disbelief. Was this the ghostly Indian Queen . . . ?

Then the flashing lights began and she realized it was a modern boat. By now Max was awake and they watched as a series of long and short flashes beamed across the bay.

"Perhaps it's a signal," said Max, as a lorry drew up on the cliff top opposite.

Sally quickly grabbed a notebook and started to scribble down the sequence, using dots for short flashes and dashes for long flashes. Max rummaged through a bag stuffed with useful equipment and pulled out his pocket codebook. He flicked through it until he found the page he was looking for and handed it to Sally.

"This will help us work out what it means," he said.

DON'T TURN THE PAGE YET

Can you decode the signal?

Watching Demon's Cove

Snatching a torch, Sally and Max hurried outside. Halfway down the steps to the cove, there was a wide ledge where they could hide and watch the beach.

A small dinghy pulled ashore. Two men clambered out and glared around, suspiciously. They began unloading some large, wooden crates. What was going on? Were they smugglers? Max leant out to get a better look and dislodged an avalanche of stones and pebbles.

They crouched down as a torch beam flashed in their direction, scanning the rock face again and again. They waited, hearts pounding, until at last a gruff voice gave the all clear.

Sally and Max stayed well hidden behind the rocks. They couldn't risk being discovered now. They heard muffled voices fading into the distance, but could see nothing. Soon there was silence and, in spite of the cold, they both felt very sleepy…

Max woke suddenly, sunlight dazzling him. He jumped to his feet, but the people and dinghy had vanished. He shook Sally and dashed down to the beach.

Max thought he caught a glimpse of the boat, but Sally was puzzled by the footprints. She could see three sets of tracks heading in one direction towards the cliff where they stopped. Someone must have rowed the dinghy away, but where had the other three people gone?

Sally stared at the cliff face, looking for a clue. She thought back to last night. Something had changed.

DON'T TURN THE PAGE YET

What has Sally noticed?

Message in a Bottle

Sally stared up towards the large boulder, sure it was hiding something. She took a deep breath and jumped onto the rocks. She scrambled up to the wide, grassy ledge with Max struggling behind.

Sally leant against the boulder and pushed. It was surprisingly light and rolled away to reveal a narrow opening. Max peered into the gloomy darkness. Sally flicked on the torch and they stepped cautiously through the gap to investigate.

They found themselves in a small cave. The torch beam disturbed some bats, but otherwise the cave was empty. Footprints in the sand matched the ones on the beach and showed that three people had walked into, but not out of, the cave. So where had they gone?

"Perhaps there's a secret tunnel," said Max.

Sally began tapping the walls, but they felt disappointingly solid. Max looked for hidden levers or buttons. But they found nothing.

Suddenly, Sally spotted a block of stone that had been firmly wedged into the wall. After a lot of tugging and a final wrench that sent Max tumbling backwards, they pulled it free and stared into the hole at an old, cobwebby bottle. Sally lifted it from its hiding place and Max pulled out a crumbly roll of paper. It was torn at the edges and faded by damp and age, but they could still see the clear outlines of a map and peculiar, sloping writing that was almost impossible to read.

DON'T TURN THE PAGE YET

Can you work out what the writing says?

Tricky Trapdoor

Sally studied the paper, thinking hard about what it meant. This was only part of a map and she wondered what had happened to the rest of it. She was sure the map was important, why else would Jago Grabbitt have hidden it so carefully? Could it have something to do with the treasure from the Indian Queen?

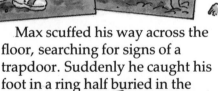

Max scuffed his way across the floor, searching for signs of a trapdoor. Suddenly he caught his foot in a ring half buried in the ground and tripped, knocking over a heavy, metal pole. He lay sprawled on the floor, but at least he knew where the trapdoor was.

Just then, Sally noticed an unusual, carved stick lying on a rock. She tucked it into her bag, then began to help Max brush away the sand from a heavy, old, oak door.

The rusty, metal ring was embedded in one side of the trapdoor. Max lifted up the ring and tugged.

Together, Sally and Max heaved, pulled and yanked, but still they couldn't lift it. The door wouldn't budge.

They gave up, this was getting them nowhere. There HAD to be another way of opening the trapdoor. Max gazed around the cave searching for inspiration, but there didn't seem to be anything that would help. Then he had a brainwave.

"This should be easy," Max exclaimed, confidently. "I know how to open it."

DON'T TURN THE PAGE YET

How can they open the trapdoor?

Into the Smugglers' Tunnels

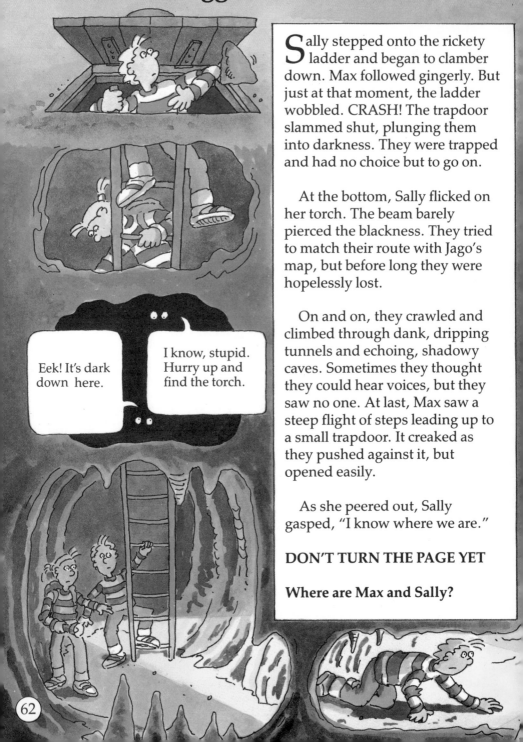

Sally stepped onto the rickety ladder and began to clamber down. Max followed gingerly. But just at that moment, the ladder wobbled. CRASH! The trapdoor slammed shut, plunging them into darkness. They were trapped and had no choice but to go on.

At the bottom, Sally flicked on her torch. The beam barely pierced the blackness. They tried to match their route with Jago's map, but before long they were hopelessly lost.

On and on, they crawled and climbed through dank, dripping tunnels and echoing, shadowy caves. Sometimes they thought they could hear voices, but they saw no one. At last, Max saw a steep flight of steps leading up to a small trapdoor. It creaked as they pushed against it, but opened easily.

As she peered out, Sally gasped, "I know where we are."

DON'T TURN THE PAGE YET

Where are Max and Sally?

Eek! It's dark down here.

I know, stupid. Hurry up and find the torch.

62

The Mystery Thickens

Silence. The cottage was deserted. Max and Sally pushed open the trapdoor and scrambled out.

They gazed at the cluttered room. Every corner and shelf was crammed with an odd assortment of curios collected from around the world. But there were also several puzzling things that seemed very unlikely possessions for a fisherman like Tom.

Suddenly, something made Sally stop and stare, a name she remembered from Tom's story of the Indian Queen.

DON'T TURN THE PAGE YET

What has Sally spotted?

65

The Old Sea Chest

Max tried the chest. It was unlocked. Sally looked doubtful; she didn't like the idea of snooping through someone else's things.

"There's something going on, and I want to find out what," said Max.

The chest was packed with mementoes from the Indian Queen – the Captain's logbook, ancient charts and old doubloons and pieces of eight . . . Max tried out the telescope, but it didn't work. He just stared into luminous, inky, blackness.

Then a recent newspaper cutting caught his eye. Max was certain he had seen the man in the photo before. He racked his brains trying to remember where.

As he read and reread the stories, a worrying suspicion began to grow in his mind. Everything that had happened started to make sense.

DON'T TURN THE PAGE YET

Where has Max seen the man before? What does he suspect?

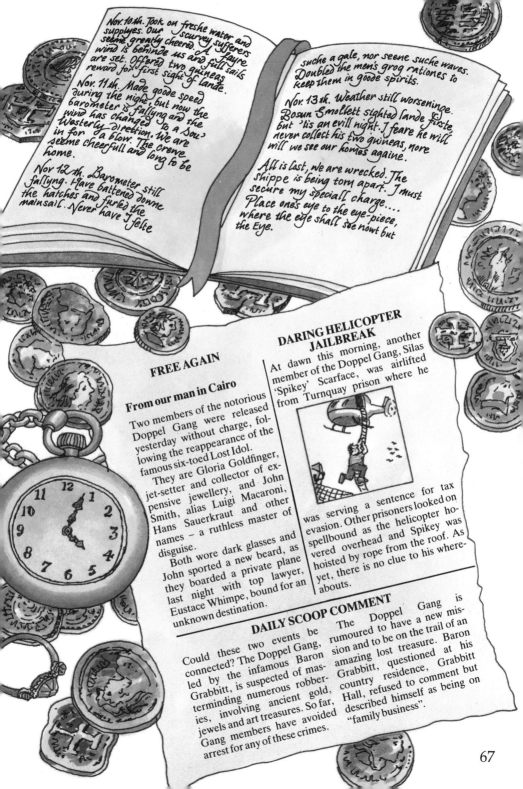

Nov. 10th. Took on freshe water and supplyes. Our scurvey sufferers seeme greatly cheered. A fayre wind is behinde us and full sails are set. Offered two guineas reward for first sight of lande.

Nov. 11th. Made goode speed during the night, but now the barometer is falling and the wind has changed to a Sou' Westerly direction. We are in for a blow. The creve seeme cheerfull and long to be home.

Nov. 12th. Barometer still falling. Have battened downe the hatches and furled the mainsail. Never have I felte

suche a gale, nor seene suche waves. Doubled the men's grog rationes to keepe them in goode spirits.

Nov. 13th. Weather still worseninge. Bosun Smollett sighted lande firste, but 'tis an evil night. I feare he will never collect his two guineas, nore will we see our homes againe.

All is lost, we are wrecked. The shippe is being torn apart. I must secure my speciall charge.... Place one's eye to the eye-piece, where the eye shall see nowt but the Eye.

FREE AGAIN

From our man in Cairo

Two members of the notorious Doppel Gang were released yesterday without charge, following the reappearance of the famous six-toed Lost Idol.

They are Gloria Goldfinger, jet-setter and collector of expensive jewellery, and John Smith, alias Luigi Macaroni, Hans Sauerkraut and other names – a ruthless master of disguise.

Both wore dark glasses and John sported a new beard, as they boarded a private plane last night with top lawyer, Eustace Whimpe, bound for an unknown destination.

DARING HELICOPTER JAILBREAK

At dawn this morning, another member of the Doppel Gang, Silas 'Spikey' Scarface, was airlifted from Turnquay prison where he

was serving a sentence for tax evasion. Other prisoners looked on spellbound as the helicopter hovered overhead and Spikey was hoisted by rope from the roof. As yet, there is no clue to his whereabouts.

DAILY SCOOP COMMENT

Could these two events be connected? The Doppel Gang, led by the infamous Baron Grabbitt, is suspected of masterminding numerous robberies, involving ancient gold, jewels and art treasures. So far, Gang members have avoided arrest for any of these crimes.

The Doppel Gang is rumoured to have a new mission and to be on the trail of an amazing lost treasure. Baron Grabbitt, questioned at his country residence, Grabbitt Hall, refused to comment but described himself as being on "family business".

Tom Acts Suspiciously

THUD THUD THUD...

Sally and Max slowly repacked the chest, their heads buzzing with unanswered questions.

Had they been watching the infamous Doppel Gang at Demon's Cove last night? Was the Gang searching for the lost treasure from the Indian Queen? And what was Tom's part in all this? It was very suspicious.

Heavy footsteps came closer and closer until they stopped outside the front door. Sally and Max watched in horror as the handle slowly turned. What should they do now? Max scooted into the open trapdoor. Sally shut the chest and dived behind the sofa, hardly daring to breathe as Tom sat down in it. She was trapped.

The silence was broken by a strange, crackling sound, followed by a high-pitched whine. Sally cautiously peeped out over the sofa as Tom leapt to his feet and rushed across to the radio.

He sat down at his desk, adjusted the radio and listened intently through the headphones. He was writing something down and seemed to be checking a notebook.

Max opened the trapdoor and saw a carved stick drop to the floor. It was the same size and just like the one Sally had picked up.

Minutes, later the door banged shut and Tom's brisk footsteps faded into the distance. Sally and Max emerged from hiding.

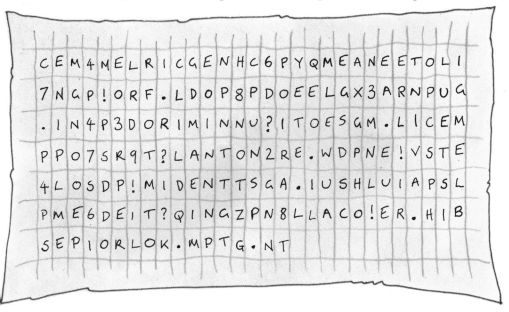

CEM4MELRICGENHC6PYQMEANEETOLI
7NGP!ORF.LDOP8PDOEELGX3ARNPUG
.IN4P3DORIMINNU?ITOE5GM.LICEM
PPO7SR9T?LANTON2RE.WDPNE!VSTE
4LOSDP!MIDENTTSGA.IUSHLUIAPSL
PME6DEIT?QINGZPN8LLACO!ER.HIB
SEPIORLOK.MPTG.NT

The paper Tom had been writing on was lying on his desk next to the radio. He had neatly written seven rows of letters on the squared paper, but they didn't appear to mean anything. Sally was totally puzzled.

"It's a code," said Max. "And I know how to read it."

DON'T TURN THE PAGE YET

What does the message say?

Looking for X

The message confirmed their worst suspicions, but where WAS the usual meeting place? Max slumped down into a chair. All their detective work seemed to have come to nothing.

Then Sally spotted Tom's notebook lying on top of the radio. It was open at a map marked with a red cross. Could this be the meeting place? It was a long shot, but it had to be worth trying. It was their only lead.

There were no labels, but Sally was sure it was a map of Nether Muckle. She and Max ran outside to the back of the cottage and stared at the village. If only they could match the map to the roads and buildings.

DON'T TURN THE PAGE YET

Can you work out which building is the one marked X on the map?

The House on the Cliff Top

Max and Sally sprinted through the village and ran on along the cliff road, past the Smuggler's Head Hotel and ruined abbey. Finally, they turned into the lane leading to the strange house on the cliff's edge.

The steep hill in front of the house made a good viewpoint. Max and Sally scrambled to the top using the thick gorse bushes as cover. Gasping for breath, they crawled to the edge and stared down at Grabbitt Hall, home of Baron Grabbitt. If this was the meeting place, they had to get inside, but finding a way in would be tricky.

DON'T TURN THE PAGE YET

Can you find a safe route into Grabbitt Hall?

GRABBITT HALL

72

Inside Grabbitt Hall

Grabbitt Hall was ominously quiet. Max and Sally sneaked downstairs and along a deserted corridor. Now they had to find out where the meeting was being held, without being discovered.

Max and Sally heard the buzz of voices ahead. They ducked behind a large suit of armour and peered out. A man was standing in the hallway giving directions to two familiar-looking people.

They waited impatiently for the man to walk slowly away down a flight of stairs and then silently tiptoed after the two visitors. Sally and Max turned into a wide, blue-carpeted corridor in time to see them disappearing through a doorway.

A minute later, Max turned the doorhandle and peeped into the room. It was empty. He looked for a door or passage, but the only door was this one. It was very strange, there HAD to be another way out. The two visitors couldn't have vanished into thin air.

Sally looked around. The walls were covered with portraits of the Baron's Grabbitt ancestors. But something was puzzling Max. Looking at one of the paintings, he could see the room had hardly changed over the years, but one thing was different. What was it?

"I've got it," Max exclaimed. "There's a secret passage, and I know where it is."

DON'T TURN THE PAGE YET

What has Max spotted? Where is the door to the secret passage?

The Round Room

Max stood face to face with the portrait of Baron Grabbitt.

"He's not very friendly," he muttered, wondering how to open the door.

Then he saw that one of the Baron's rings had a button where the jewel should have been.

There was a loud whirring as Max touched the button. The Baron slid slowly aside to reveal an eerie, wood-panelled passage, lit only by candlelight. There was no one around, so Max and Sally tiptoed in, not knowing what, or who, to expect. It was a bit spooky, but they reached the open door at the end, unchallenged.

They peeped into a deserted room. Sally glanced around nervously. Where had the two visitors gone? She spotted some scattered papers and part of an ancient-looking map on the table.

"Property of Den . . . it must be Denzil Grabbitt," Sally exclaimed, reading the bottom line of writing.

She delved into her rucksack and pulled out Jago's map. She knew it would match Denzil's. Max whipped out his new, mini camera. CLICK and the picture was taken.

"Now we've got a copy of the map and no one will know we've been here," he said, stuffing the camera into his pocket. "Let's go."

Sally was looking at the map. There was still one piece missing, but she was sure the writing would give them a clue to where the treasure was hidden.

The writing on Denzil's map was very strange, but as she stared it began to make sense.

DON'T TURN THE PAGE YET

What is written on the map?

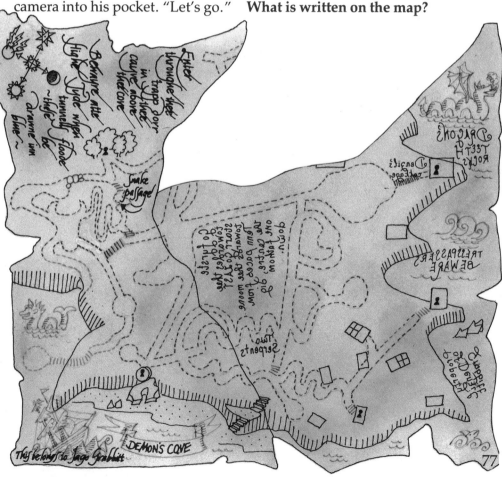

Trapped

There was an ominous scraping sound. A panel opened revealing another room and gloomy passage. Framed in the doorway stood Baron Grabbitt and the Doppel Gang.

"I'll take that," the Baron snarled, snatching the map from Max. "We've been watching you sneaking through the Hall on the TV screen."

Max groaned. Closed circuit television; they should have guessed. He looked around, but they were surrounded with no hope of escape. Sally watched miserably as the lady with orange hair studied their map. At least they still had the camera and film. Spikey grabbed Max and a man called Harry pushed Sally towards the dark passage.

They were marched down a flight of wide, stone stairs and through a huge cave to a long passageway. Harry hurried them straight on, ignoring the tunnels on either side, until they came to seven steep steps.

At the bottom they turned left and carried on into a small, round cave. Even Sally had to duck as she stepped into the low tunnel that twisted down and down. There were more steps, but these were so wet and slippery that Sally, who was trying to memorize their route, lost count.

Finally they came to a small, damp cave where the two men left them tied up. Max wriggled across to some jagged rocks and began to saw at the rope around his wrists. Luckily, it was easy to cut. Meanwhile, Sally had worked out where they were and was trying to find the best route out of the caves, avoiding Grabbitt Hall. Her brilliant memory meant she could picture the map clearly.

DON'T TURN THE PAGE YET

Where are they? Which is the shortest route out, avoiding Grabbitt Hall?

79

Escape through the Tunnels

Sally and Max ran so quickly, they were gasping for breath by the time they reached the Snake Passage. But at least there was no danger of being followed here. The tunnel was so narrow, it was a tight squeeze even for Max and Sally.

At last they came to a wider passage which sloped steeply upwards towards a small wooden door. But as Max fumbled with the catch, they heard footsteps, running. A tall figure loomed suddenly from the dark shadows behind them.

DETECTIVE INSPECTOR
THOMAS CLIPPER
T Clipper
Special Undercover Agent

"I thought I'd never catch you," a gruff voice wheezed.

Tom! They were trapped. Max shoved against the door, trying desperately to open it. Then Tom whisked out a plastic identity card.

"We thought..." Sally began.

". . . I was one of the Doppel Gang," Tom finished. "I realized that. I came to rescue you and guessed you would make for here, but I had to go the long way round."

They set off at once for Tom's cottage where he could develop their film. As they scrambled out and made their way through the wood and across the fields, Tom told them the rest of the story.

The Grabbitts made an ingenious plan to hide the treasure, until the hunt for it had been called off.

They hid it in the confusing maze of tunnels at Demon's Cove and drew a map to show the hiding place.

But the brothers didn't trust each other so they divided the map into three parts. Each wrote a vital clue on his portion. When they died, the map was forgotten.

I'm very interested in the case of the Indian Queen treasure, as Captain Clipper is my great great great grandfather.

Baron Grabbitt is Denzil's great great grandson. Gloria Goldfinger discovered Denzil's map while going through some of his old books.

I have been trailing the Gang for months, investigating their activities.

This is how the Doppel Gang's hunt for the treasure and for the missing parts of the map began.

Photo Identification

Tom led Sally and Max into a tumbledown barn behind his cottage. They gazed around in amazement. Inside, the barn was transformed into a high-tech office. Tom opened an important-looking box marked "Police File". It was packed with photographs.

"I want you to help with evidence," Tom explained, making Max and Sally feel very important. "Pick out every photo showing members of the Doppel Gang."

Tom disappeared into the darkroom with their film while Max and Sally spread out the photos. He particularly wanted them to identify the two new gang members. At first it seemed impossible, but they soon spotted familiar faces and some which were cleverly disguised. They could also name most of them.

DON'T TURN THE PAGE YET

Find all the photos of the Doppel Gang and name as many as you can.

THE DOPPEL GANG:
BARON GRABBITT Millionaire, Gang leader. Power-crazy, highly dangerous.
GLORIA GOLDFINGER The brains of the Gang. Tall, slim and vain. Can't resist expensive jewellery. Often changes hair colour.
JOHN SMITH Now known as Harry Loimeswolde. (Other aliases: Luigi Macaroni, Angus McHaggis.) Ruthless master of disguise. Small scar on left jaw.
SILAS 'SPIKEY' SCARFACE Expert thief. Left leg shorter than right leg. Scar on right cheek.
EUSTACE WHIMPE The Gang's lawyer. Short, skinny and weedy.
+ TWO RECENT RECRUITS

SWINDELLS BANK
Lutzdorn, Switzerland
NAME: GRABBITT (Baron)
FORENAMES: Brian Archibald
ADDRESS: GRABBITT HALL
Nether Muckle.
ACCOUNT NO: AX 12345

The Missing Link

Tom studied the photos of the two new Gang members and frowned.

"Fingers Golightly and Dinah Might. Notorious villains," he said.

Tom held out the newly-developed print showing the two portions of the treasure map. He locked the barn and led Sally and Max across the garden towards his cottage.

As he opened the back door, all three heard a suspicious, scuffling noise.

They were just in time to see a man disappear through the front door.

Tom glanced across at his safe. It was open and he knew it was empty.

Sally dashed to the window and saw Spikey running towards a van. He was brandishing a small piece of paper. The engine revved, Spikey jumped inside and the van roared away.

Tom lifted down a dusty tin.

"The Doppel Gang must know who I am," he said. "They've taken my copy. But . . . I've still got the original."

Copy? Original? What was Tom talking about? He took a small scrap of yellowing paper from the tin. It was the third piece of the Grabbitt brothers' map.

"But how did you find it?" asked Sally, not quite believing her eyes.

This portion of the map had belonged to Joshua Grabbitt, the youngest of the brothers. For Tom was not only descended from Captain Clipper, but also from Joshua Grabbitt. The Captain's grandson had married Joshua's grandaughter. Just last week, Tom had found the map rolled up and forgotten in the attic along with Captain Clipper's chest. Now they could work out where the treasure was hidden. But they would have to move fast to get there before the Doppel Gang.

DON'T TURN THE PAGE YET

Can you work out where the treasure is hidden?

Treasure from the Indian Queen

They raced out to Tom's jeep and set off. Tom radioed for reinforcements and the jeep lurched down the gravel track. With Max in the lead, they scrambled through the trapdoor and down into the maze of dark tunnels, to the Demon's Lair. The Doppel Gang had yet to arrive.

Large boulders made a screen around one side of the cave. It was impossible to hear anyone approaching because it was high tide and the sound of the sea roaring in the tunnels echoed through the cave. Tom found a good hiding place where they could keep watch. They switched off their torch and waited.

It was not long before Max spotted a torch beam. The Doppel Gang marched into the cave. Harry counted ten paces from the centre and the Gang set to work with spades, while Gloria and the Baron watched.

At last there was a shout, the Gang had found the treasure. It was time to put Tom's plan into action. The special microwave radio crackled to life. As Tom struggled to hear what was being said, he turned very pale and began to look very worried.

"There's been a delay," he whispered. "The plan won't work. We only have enough men to guard one tunnel and there are four exits from the cave."

Sally's mind whizzed into action. She thought back to the plan of the caves and realized there WAS only one way out. Sally, Max and Tom edged their way out of the cave, while the Gang were busy with the chests. Tom radioed his instructions.

DON'T TURN THE PAGE YET

Is Sally right? Which exit should they guard?

The Demon's Eye Diamond

The plan was a success. Almost before Max and Sally knew it, the six members of the Doppel Gang were safely in police custody. Tom, Max and Sally followed as the Gang were led through the tunnels to Demon's Cove, where a police launch was waiting. Outside on the beach, Tom opened the chests. Max and Sally gazed in amazement at the treasure. But they quickly realized something was wrong. The red leather box that should have held the Demon's Eye diamond was empty.

Had one of the Doppel Gang secretly taken it? Sally didn't think so. She was convinced the Grabbitt brothers had never found the famous jewel all those years ago. But if she was right, where was it now? Sally remembered Captain Clipper's logbook, she knew that it held the answer.

DON'T TURN THE PAGE YET

Where is the Demon's Eye diamond?

88

Clues

Pages 54-55

Look at Max's codebook. Each group of dots and dashes stands for a letter.

Pages 56-57

This is easy. Use your eyes.

Pages 58-59

The letters are written in old-fashioned English. Some words are spelt strangely.

Pages 60-61

Look carefully at all the things in the cave.

Pages 62-63

Look back through the book. Do you recognize anything?

Pages 64-65

This is easy. Use your eyes.

Pages 66-67

Look back at the people on page 56.

Pages 68-69

The carved stick Sally picked up on page 60 will help.

Pages 70-71

Try turning the map the other way up. Work out where Tom's cottage is first.

Pages 72-73

They can crawl behind bushes and walls to keep out of sight. Are there any open windows or doors?

Pages 74-75

This is easy. Compare the room as it is now to the same room in one of the paintings.

Pages 76-77

The clues on this page give you a clue to Denzil's writing.

Pages 78-79

Look back at the two pieces of map. Grabbit Hall was built on the site of Denzil's cottage.

Pages 82-83

Use your eyes and remember what you have learnt about members of the Doppel Gang.

Pages 84-85

Look at all the clues on the map and try putting them into order.

Pages 86-87

You may need to look back at the map on the previous page.

Page 88

Carefully read Captain Clipper's logbook on page 67.

Answers

Pages 54-55

The message is in morse code. This is what it says:

Diving party landing with equipment and wreckage from Indian Queen. Standby to receive at Demon's Cove. End of message.

Pages 56-57

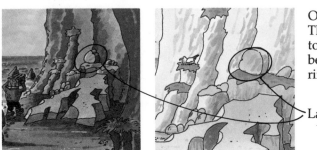

One thing has changed. The large boulder on top of the ledge has been turned round. It is ringed in both pictures.

Large boulder

Pages 58-59

The letters are written in an old-fashioned way and where the letter s comes in the middle of a word, it is written like an f. Some words are also spelt differently.
This is what it says:

Enter through the trapdoor in the cave above the Cove.

This keyhole symbol shows there is a door.

Beware at high tide when tunnels flood – they be drawn in blue.

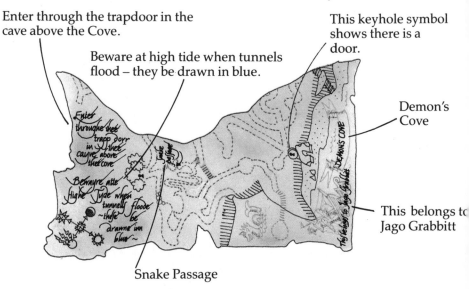

Demon's Cove

This belongs to Jago Grabbitt

Snake Passage

Pages 60-61

They open the trapdoor using the metal pole Max knocked over as a lever. They balance the pole on top of the rock which then acts as a pivot.

This means they need less effort and strength to open the door.
These diagrams show how Max and Sally open the trapdoor.

The pole is pushed through the ring

Metal pole lever

Pivot rock

They push here to lift open the trapdoor

Pages 62-63

The trapdoor opens into Tom's cottage. Sally knows this because she spots the stained glass window which she saw from the outside on page 53.

Stained glass window

Pages 64-65

Sally has spotted the name Captain T. Clipper on the sea chest. He was captain of the Indian Queen. You can see the name ringed here.

The other puzzling things Max and Sally have noticed are labelled.

Gun in holster

Powerful binoculars

Radio transceiver

Camera and lenses

Pistol

Pages 66-67

Max saw the man in the photo last night. He was one of the people on the beach at Demon's Cove.

Here is the man from the photo.

Max suspects the Doppel Gang are looking for the lost treasure from the Indian Queen. His main reasons are: the Doppel Gang's interest in ancient treasure; the message Max and Sally decoded on page 55; the fact that

Baron Grabbit, the Gang leader, has the same surname as the Grabbit brothers who wrecked the Indian Queen.

Pages 68-69

Max decodes the message using the carved stick that Sally found on page 60. Place the stick below each line of writing. Lines on the stick match the letters on the paper. To break the code, read the letters which are above notches on the stick.

Here is the message:

Emergency meeting of Doppel Gang in 30 minutes. Important new developments. Usual meeting place. Be prompt.

Pages 70-71

The building marked X on the map is ringed in black.

Tom's cottage is here.

The safe route into Grabbitt Hall is marked in black.

Pages 74-75

In the painting above the fireplace, Max spotted a door where the life-size portrait of Baron Grabbitt now hangs. The entrance to the hidden passage must be behind this picture.

This is the door Max spotted.

The door is behind this portrait.

Pages 76-77

The words on Denzil's portion of the map are written backwards. This is what it says:

Two Serpents

Go First towards the star.
Go Last towards the moon. Ten paces from the centre, dig one fathom down.

Denzil's cottage

Dragon's Teeth Rocks

Trespassers beware. Property of Denzil Grabbitt

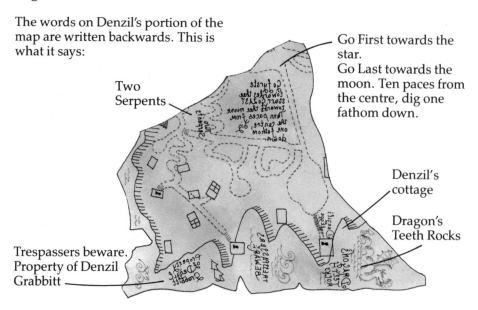

Pages 78-79

The shortest way out is marked in black.

Sally and Max are here.

Here you can see the members of the Doppel Gang.

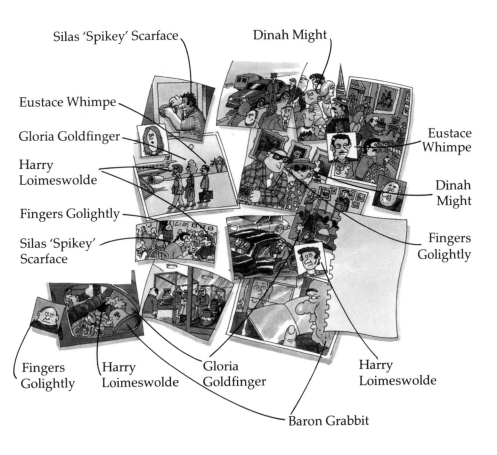

Silas 'Spikey' Scarface

Dinah Might

Eustace Whimpe

Gloria Goldfinger

Harry Loimeswolde

Fingers Golightly

Silas 'Spikey' Scarface

Eustace Whimpe

Dinah Might

Fingers Golightly

Fingers Golightly

Harry Loimeswolde

Gloria Goldfinger

Harry Loimeswolde

Baron Grabbit

Written in order, the clues say:
Enter through the trapdoor in the cave above the Cove. (Map page 59)
Go First towards the star. (Map page 77).
Second, look left from the Brigand's Boot and then descend the stair; steer by the comet into the Demon's Lair. (Map page 85).

Go Last towards the moon. Ten paces from the centre, dig one fathom down. (Map page 77.)

(One fathom is equal to six feet.)

You can see where the treasure is buried on the completed map, shown on the next page.

The treasure is buried here.

The Grabbitt brothers' route to the treasure is marked here in black.

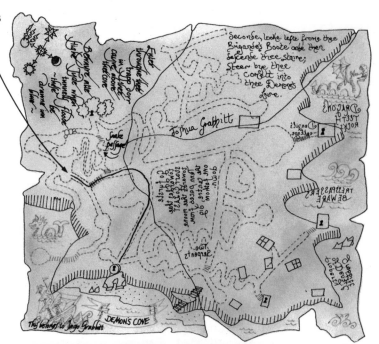

Pages 86-87

Sally is right.
This is the only tunnel that must be guarded.

It is high tide and so this tunnel is flooded.

This tunnel is blocked.

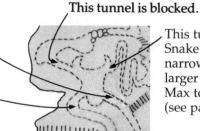

This tunnel leads to the Snake Passage. It is too narrow for anyone larger than Sally and Max to squeeze through (see page 80).

Page 88

Read the last entry in Captain Clipper's logbook on page 67. This tells you the Demon's Eye diamond is hidden in the telescope which Max tries to look through on page 66.

You can see the diamond gleaming here.

THE INCREDIBLE DINOSAUR EXPEDITION

Karen Dolby

Illustrated by Brenda Haw

Designed by Patrick Knowles

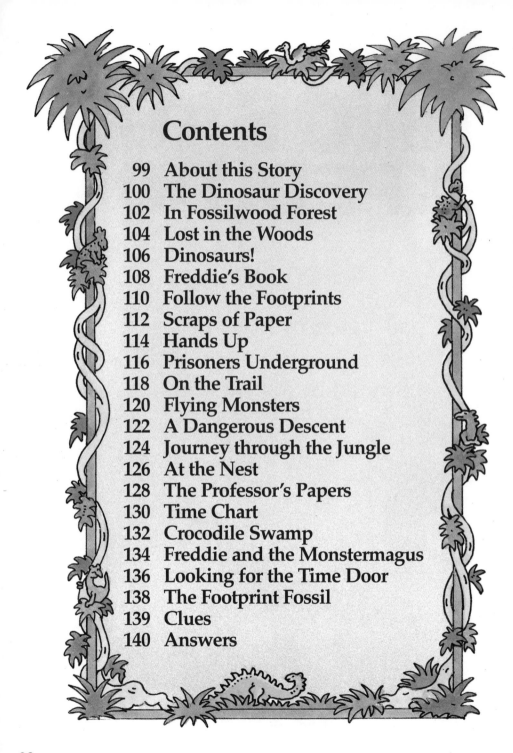

Contents

About this Story

The Incredible Dinosaur Expedition is an action-packed adventure story that takes you backwards in time to the eerie, unknown world of the dinosaurs.

Along the way, there are lots of fun puzzles and tricky problems to solve. Find the answers to these before going on to the next episode in the story.

Look at the pictures carefully and watch out for vital clues and information. Sometimes you will need to flick back through the story to help you find the answer.

There are extra clues on page 139 and you can check your answers on pages 140 to 144.

Just turn the page to begin the adventure...

The Dinosaur Discovery

Freddie was bored, so bored that he had even lent Jo his roller skates. He munched his way through a bumper bag of banana toffees and wished that something exciting would happen.

Just then, Freddie's friend, Zack, zoomed up on his skateboard.

"Come and read this," Zack yelled, waving a very crumpled newspaper page.

"But newspapers are so boring," Freddie groaned, aiming a toffee at Zack's head.

"There's been the most amazing dinosaur discovery," said Zack, ignoring Freddie.

"And it's near here," Jo exclaimed, staring at the page. "In Fossilwood Forest."

"Let's go," said Zack. "Maybe WE can find some dinosaur bones."

Freddie groaned again and carried on munching. But two toffees later he set off after Zack and Jo.

On the right you can read Zack's newspaper.

Jo

Zack

Freddie

~DAILY SCOOP~

AMAZING DINOSAUR DISCOVERY
...it's a monster mystery

by Ivor Lead

Late last night, the most incredible dinosaur discovery EVER was made in Fossilwood Forest.

A team of dinosaur experts led by Professor Cuthbert Crank-Pott have found a whole dinosaur skeleton, of a type never seen before.

MONSTERMAGUS

Professor Crank-Pott has named this amazing dinosaur MONSTERMAGUS. In an exclusive interview earlier today, he described the monster.

"This dinosaur was huge – 15 metres tall with large, sharp claws on its feet. It must have devoured enormous amounts of flesh every day and makes Tyrannosaurus Rex look as fierce as a baby hamster."

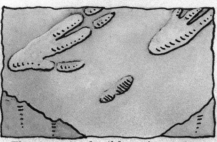

These amazing fossil footprints were found beneath the dinosaur skeleton. The large prints belong to the Monstermagus, but the little one is a mystery. It looks like a human shoeprint.

Humans and dinosaurs never lived on earth together . . . or did they?

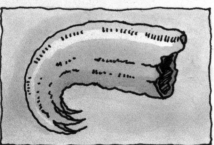

This three-spiked claw belonged to the Monstermagus. It had two of them, one on each of its feet. Experts believe they were used for spearing its prey. So far only one of them has been found.

MYSTERIOUS CLAIMS

On top of his startling skeleton discovery, Professor Crank-Pott claims that he has found a method of hatching live dinosaurs from prehistoric eggs!

He refuses to reveal the secret of his discovery but promises to show the world the results.

Is this really possible? No one knows for sure. A rival expert, Dr Noel Knowall says the Professor's claims are "crazy" "daft" "mad" and "impossible". We shall have to wait and see . . .

Professor Crank-Pott

FOSSILWOOD FOREST LONG AGO

150 million years ago, dinosaurs roamed what is now Fossilwood Forest. No one knows what the landscape looked like then. Some experts say it was a marshy swamp, others think the land was dotted with erupting volcanoes. The Monstermagus and the footprint fossils were buried in a layer of volcanic lava, but nearby, experts have found fossils of shells and prehistoric crocodiles.

In Fossilwood Forest

Half an hour later they stumbled into a clearing in Fossilwood Forest. This was the site of the dinosaur discovery, but it wasn't at all what they expected.

"It looks just like a rubbish dump," moaned Freddie.

Zack and Jo pulled out their spades and started searching through the rubbish for dinosaur bones. Freddie found a comfortable spot beneath a tree and pulled out something plastic and stripey.

"What's that?" cried Zack.

"My inflatable air cushion, of course," said Freddie.

Then, to Zack and Jo's amazement, he blew up the air cushion and sat down with his pocket dinosaur book and a mammoth bar of chocolate.

Jo chucked a slithery earthworm in Freddie's direction and carried on scrabbling in the rubbish. All of a sudden, she spotted something.

"Look! Look over there," she cried in an excited voice. "It's the Monstermagus claw!"

Can you find the missing Monstermagus claw?

Lost in the Woods

Very carefully, Jo prised the claw out of the ground. She wrapped it in Freddie's empty toffee bag and put it in her rucksack.

"Let's go home," Freddie said as a raindrop trickled down his neck. "I'm getting wet and this wood is starting to give me the creeps."

The other two agreed. They had to make their way to Forest Lane. But which way was it?

"I know," said Jo. "Take the left fork at the well and . . ."

"No," said Zack. "It's straight on at the well and across the crossroads. First left, first right, right again and first left. Over the bridge and we're there. Easy."

"Wrong," said Jo. "Left at the well and straight on at Hangman's Cross. Follow the path round past the track to Spring Cottage, turn left at the end and take the second path on the right. Then follow the long, wiggly path to Forest Lane."

"You're both wrong," said Freddie. "We go right at Hangman's Cross, follow the path over the bridge, turn second left, then first left and Forest Lane is at the end."

They chose Zack's route and as they walked on through the forest the sky grew darker.

Where does Zack's route take them?
Whose route is correct?

St Elmo's Church

Lizard Rock

Stony Brook

Ruined Cottage

Wild Woods

Marlpit

Stone Barn

Old Well

Haunted House

Dinosaurs!

All of a sudden they saw a patch of bright light ahead. They hurried towards it and stepped out into hot, hazy sunshine.

Jo stared in amazement. The forest had become a jungle. A giant dragonfly whizzed past Zack's nose and Freddie shrieked as a large, slimy slug slid over his shoes.

But most terrifying of all, were the strange roars and crashes, coming closer and closer. Zack made a gap in the leaves and peered through.

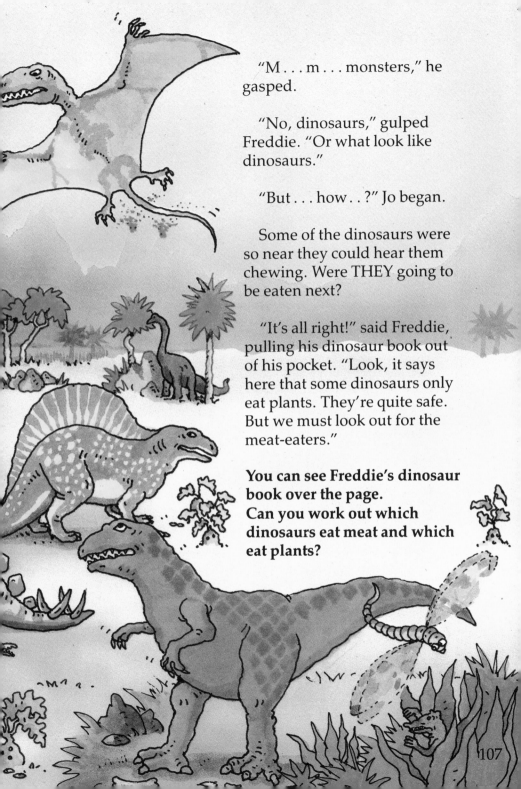

"M . . . m . . . monsters," he gasped.

"No, dinosaurs," gulped Freddie. "Or what look like dinosaurs."

"But . . . how . . ?" Jo began.

Some of the dinosaurs were so near they could hear them chewing. Were THEY going to be eaten next?

"It's all right!" said Freddie, pulling his dinosaur book out of his pocket. "Look, it says here that some dinosaurs only eat plants. They're quite safe. But we must look out for the meat-eaters."

**You can see Freddie's dinosaur book over the page.
Can you work out which dinosaurs eat meat and which eat plants?**

Freddie's Book

Dinosaurs

Dinosaurs were a group of creatures who lived on earth for 135 million years. They died out over 60 million years before man appeared.

Tyrannosaurus Rex

The word dinosaur means "terrible lizard". There were lots of different types of dinosaurs and we know what they looked like from fossils, although we don't know what colour they were.

Fossils

A fossil is the remains of an animal or plant preserved in stone. There are fossils of dinosaur bones, eggs, teeth and claws. There are even fossils of their footprints and skin.

A dinosaur became a fossil if its body was buried quickly. This was most likely to happen if it died near water. You can find out how this happened below.

How Fossils Were Made

When a dinosaur died near a swamp or river its body sank into the mud at the bottom. There its flesh rotted away, leaving the skeleton.

Layers of mud, sand and gravel built up. Then chemicals from the water entered the dinosaur's bones, slowly turning the skeleton into rock.

Movements in the earth's crust shift rock containing fossils to the surface. Wind and rain wear away the rock and uncover part of the fossil.

Footprints

Megalosaurus

Fossil footprints were made when a dinosaur walked on mud which was baked hard by the sun and covered by sand. Slowly this turned into rock with the footprint tracks still in it.

What Dinosaurs Ate

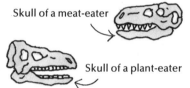

Skull of a meat-eater

Skull of a plant-eater

Some dinosaurs ate meat – they had sharp, pointed teeth. Others ate plants – they had flat, grinding teeth and some had bony beaks.

Bony plates

Spikes

Plant-eaters had to protect themselves from meat-eaters. Some plant-eaters had spikes or bony plates on their bodies, others stayed in herds.

Big and Small

Diplodocus

Compsognathus

Diplodocus was one of the biggest dinosaurs, measuring 28 metres from its head to the tip of its tail. It ate plants and stayed in herds.

The smallest dinosaur, called *Compsognathus,* was only the size of a crow. It ran very fast and ate insects and small reptiles.

Baby Dinosaurs

Baby *Protoceratops*

Most dinosaurs laid eggs. These were buried, or laid in a hollow "nest" in the ground. Fossils of *Protoceratops* eggs, like the ones above, have been found with baby dinosaur bones inside. The babies looked just like small adults.

Follow the Footprints

Zack and Jo didn't wait to look at Freddie's dinosaur book. They turned round and ran back through the bushes, retracing their steps. Freddie followed. Their footprints were clear enough, but everything else was different. Where were they?

"We must have walked through a time warp," Freddie said cheerfully.

"WHAT?" cried Zack and Jo together.

"I think we've travelled backwards in time . . . to the age of the dinosaurs," Freddie explained.

"But they're the wrong colour for dinosaurs," said Jo.

"How do you know?" asked Freddie.

They walked on in silence. Zack and Jo tried hard to find another explanation, but they couldn't think of one.

"But how did it happen?" asked Jo. "I don't understand. What did we do?"

No one knew. Jo stopped suddenly. There was something odd about the tracks on the ground.

What has Jo seen?

Scraps of Paper

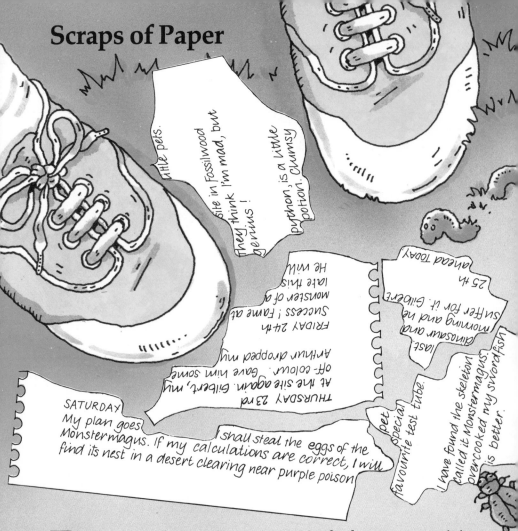

F urther on in the jungle, Freddie noticed some torn-up scraps of paper lying in the grass. Each one was covered in black, spidery writing. He picked them up and pieced them together like a jigsaw puzzle.

"It's a page from somebody's diary," Jo exclaimed.

"And whoever wrote it is here with us now," added Zack, looking at the bottom of the page. "The last date is August 25th. That's today."

Piece together the scraps of paper to find out what is written in the diary.

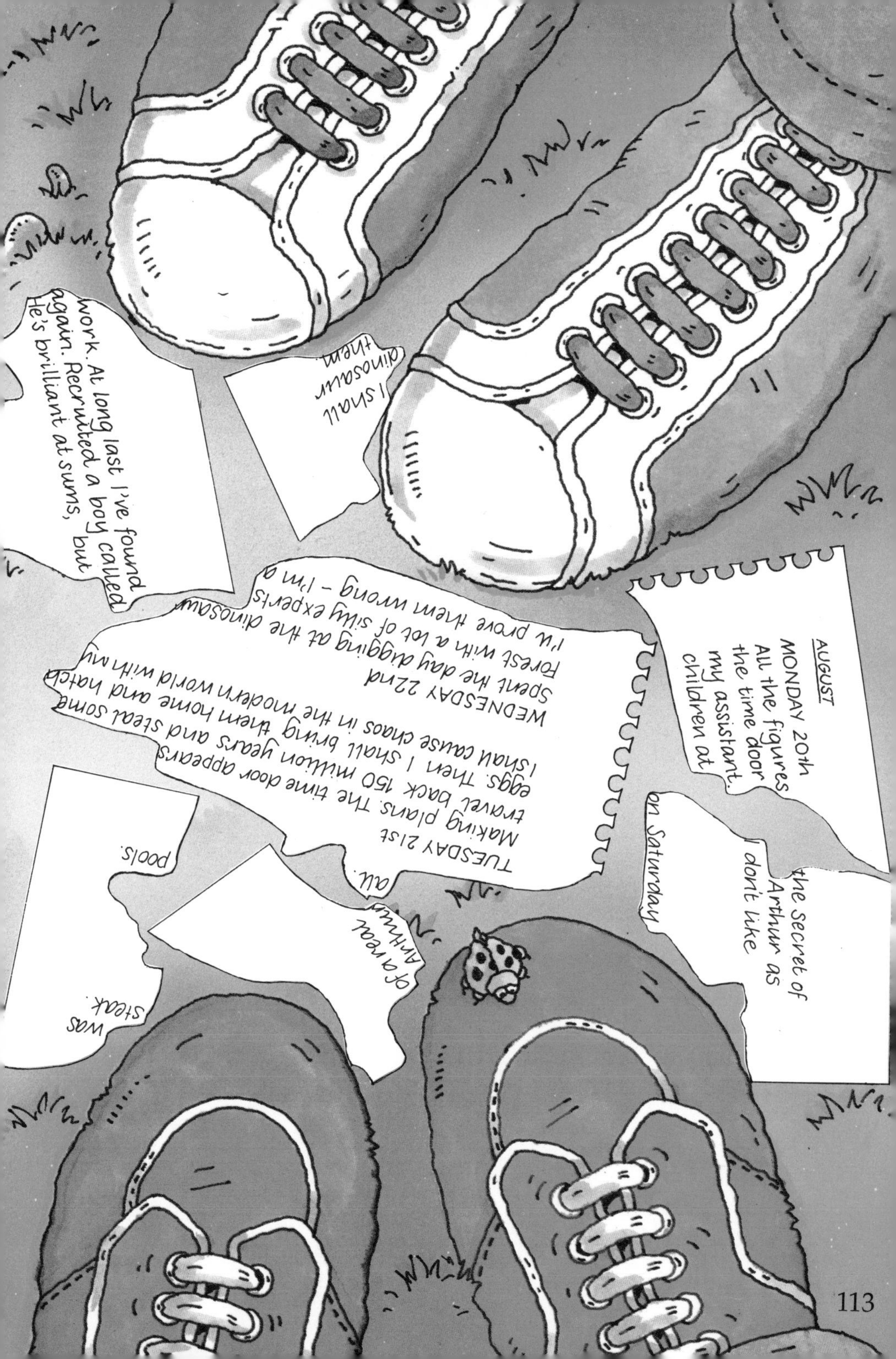

work. At long last I've found
again. Recruited a boy called
He's brilliant at sums, but

I shall dinosaur them.

WEDNESDAY 22nd
Spent the day digging at the dinosaur
forest with a lot of silly experts – I'm a
I'll prove them wrong –

TUESDAY 21st
Making plans. The time door appears. I shall
travel back 150 million years and steal some
eggs. Then I shall bring them home and hatch
them home in the modern world with my
I shall cause chaos in the modern world with my

MONDAY 20th
ALL the figures
the time door
my assistant.
children at

on Saturday

the secret of
Arthur as
don't like

of a real
Arthur.

was
steak.
pools.

113

Hands Up

Freddie was worried. Whoever wrote the diary had some very weird ideas.

"I think we should watch out," he said.

"So you should," answered a sinister voice. "Hands up!"

They looked up – straight into the barrel of a shot gun. At the other end was a white-haired man wearing a bow tie.

"What are you doing here?" demanded the man. "That's MY diary and you've walked through MY time door."

Then he shouted at the miserable-looking boy standing beside him. Jo gasped in surprise. It was Arthur, star of the school science club.

"It's all your fault Arthur," yelled the man. "Tie these spies up at once."

Arthur looked even more miserable, but he did as he was told. Jo tried to speak to him, but he wouldn't look at her.

The man prodded Freddie in the back with the barrel of his gun and ordered them to move. He marched them along at break-neck speed, deeper and deeper into the thick, tropical jungle. Curious eyes stared out at them from the undergrowth.

Large drops of rain splashed down and mud squelched under their feet. But still they walked on . . . and on.

Zack glanced back at the man. His face was very familiar. He was sure he had seen him before.

Do you know who the man is? What is his name?

115

Prisoners Underground

The Professor stopped suddenly. Ahead lay a large hole in the ground.

"Stop!" barked the Professor. "This is the end of the road for you three meddlesome brats."

He dragged Zack by the scruff of his neck and pushed him down into the hole. Then he grabbed Jo.

"Down you go," he sneered. "You should make very interesting fossils."

When Freddie's turn came something strange happened. The Professor turned away for a split second and Arthur thrust a scrap of paper into his hand. But there was no time to look at it. Freddie skidded down the hole and along a dark, wet tunnel. Then he felt himself falling down and down into the darkness.

He landed on a mound of soft earth, next to Zack and Jo. They were sitting in a shadowy, underground cave. It was cold, dark and wet. What were they going to do?

Freddie unfolded Arthur's note. He wanted to help them! But first they had to find a way out of the cave. Zack tried climbing up to the tunnel, but he was pushed back by a stream of water pouring into the cave. There was a hole in the roof, but it was too high to reach.

By now, the tunnel stream had become a torrent and water was splashing around their ankles . . . and their knees. They had to find a way out FAST or they would drown.

In a flash of inspiration, Freddie realized he had something that would save their lives and help them to escape from the cave.

How can they escape?

117

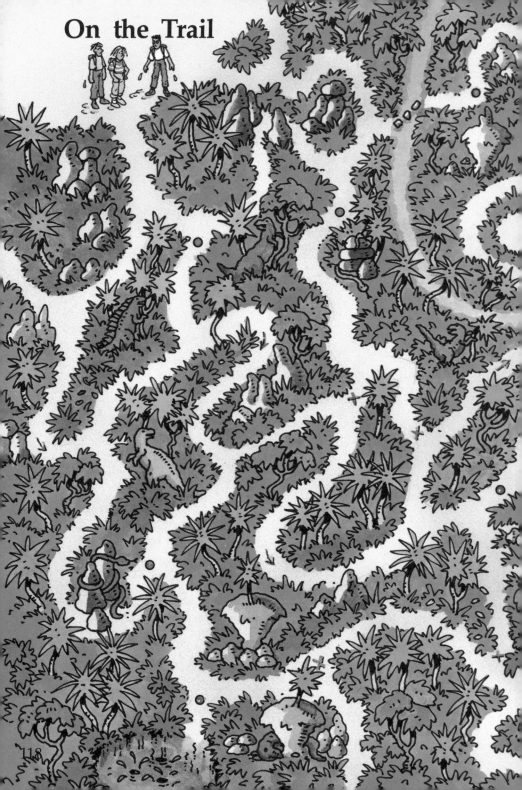

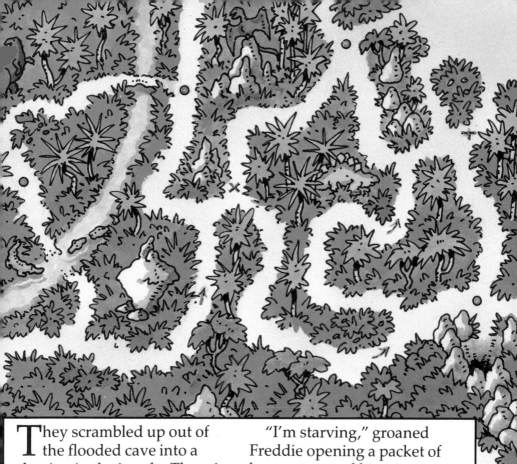

They scrambled up out of the flooded cave into a clearing in the jungle. The rain had stopped and their clothes began to dry in the sunshine. They looked around for Arthur's trail.

"Can we trust him?" asked Zack uncertainly.

They had no choice. Arthur was the only one who could lead them to the Professor. And without the Professor, there was no chance of getting home.

"I'm starving," groaned Freddie opening a packet of banana custard biscuits.

Jo pulled a face at Freddie, but Zack took no notice. His eyes scanned the ground. He set off along a narrow track leading deep into the jungle. A little way on, he spotted three twigs in the shape of an arrow. It was the start of Arthur's trail.

Can you follow Arthur's trail through the jungle?

Flying Monsters

At the edge of the jungle, they heard a loud wooshing noise. All around, the trees began to rustle. They looked up and saw an enormous flying dinosaur.

"It's a Pteranodon," said Freddie in a know-all voice.

The Pteranodon swooped down and seized Jo and Freddie in its sharp claws. Then it opened its beak and grabbed Zack by his collar. It soared above the jungle, away from the trail, and dropped them on a high rocky crag.

"I think we're next on the menu," Zack gulped.

But just as the dinosaur opened its giant beak, a shadow fell across the rock. An even bigger monster appeared in the sky flying towards them.

"It's a Quetzalcoatlus!" shrieked Freddie.

It dived, screeching, at the Pteranodon and the two monsters flew into battle. Jo crossed her fingers and shut her eyes tight . . .

When she opened them again, the monsters had gone. They were safe, but they had lost Arthur's trail. How would they find the Professor and the Monstermagus nest now?

Zack had an idea. He pulled out his pocket compass. North was directly behind him.

Where is the nest?

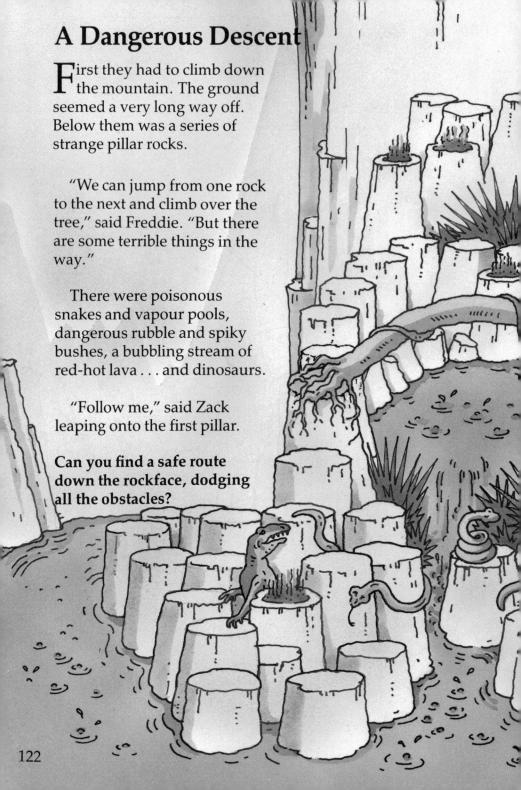

A Dangerous Descent

First they had to climb down the mountain. The ground seemed a very long way off. Below them was a series of strange pillar rocks.

"We can jump from one rock to the next and climb over the tree," said Freddie. "But there are some terrible things in the way."

There were poisonous snakes and vapour pools, dangerous rubble and spiky bushes, a bubbling stream of red-hot lava . . . and dinosaurs.

"Follow me," said Zack leaping onto the first pillar.

Can you find a safe route down the rockface, dodging all the obstacles?

Journey through the Jungle

Keeping the blue-capped volcano in sight, they headed off through the unknown jungle. All around, they could hear strange noises and rustlings. They stopped abruptly. Straight ahead, was a dinosaur the size of an elephant.

"It's an Allosaurus," said Freddie, cheerfully. "Where's my camera? Imagine him next to Dad in my photo album."

Neither Zack nor Jo wanted to hang about taking photos. They turned and dashed away. Freddie followed . . . and so did the Allosaurus.

They ran at full pelt until they were ready to drop, but the dinosaur showed no signs of slowing up. Suddenly Zack stopped under a tall tree. He jumped up, grabbed a sturdy branch and hauled himself up. Jo and Freddie did the same.

You urv ern yeat rhn
eesd. Ton'w torra ybout
thm eonstermagut.
Shp erofessor'd sarw
tilp lui tt ts oleef poo
rnh eouy. Roc uaf nint
dht eimd eooro st nhp
erofessor't simc
ehari – tt'a so nlt,
dorr nolo lp fapet
riew dito hnr eer
dibbon.

Perched up high among the leaves, they felt safe. The Allosaurus paused below them and looked up. It snarled and gnashed its teeth, but it couldn't reach them.

At last it walked on. They waited until it was out of sight before climbing back down to the ground. Then Jo spotted the crumpled piece of paper pinned to a tree trunk.

"We must be back on Arthur's trail," she cried excitedly.

Jo unpinned the paper and groaned. The message was in code.

"I can't work it out at all," she said. "You two have a look."

Can you decode Arthur's message?

At the Nest

They crept on. It wasn't far now. The clearing lay straight ahead and in the distance, they could see the steaming poison pools.

All of a sudden, Zack saw the Professor. He was standing in a hollow beside eight large, white eggs. Behind him lay an enormous, sleeping dinosaur. It was the Monstermagus.

They ducked behind a boulder and watched the Professor lift the eggs out of the nest. He examined them one by one.

"He's stealing the eggs," gasped Freddie. "We've got to stop him."

But there was nothing they could do. The Professor laid the eggs in a large metal chest, closed the lid and tapped some buttons on the top. Then he called to Arthur and marched off briskly towards the blue-capped volcano carrying only a camera and tripod.

"It's our big chance," said Zack. "Quickly! Let's take the eggs."

If they replaced the eggs with stones, the Professor would never know they were gone. But there was one problem. The box was locked.

"It's a combination lock," said Jo, looking at the buttons on the lid. "You press certain buttons in a special order to unlock it."

Some buttons were numbered, others were blank. Which ones should they press?

Then Freddie noticed a scrap of paper lying beside the metal chest. There was a list of confusing instructions written on it.

"These might help," he said, reading the first one aloud.

Which buttons should they press to open the box? You will need to find the missing numbers first.

Each row and diagonal adds up to 15.

The buttons are numbered 1 to 9.

Press the evens to open and the odds to close, in ascending order.

The Professor's Papers

Freddie carefully lifted the eggs out of the chest and Zack carried them back to the nest. The Monstermagus was still sleeping peacefully. Jo filled the chest with stones and locked it again.

"Now we've got to find the Professor's time chart," she said.

Freddie started emptying the Professor's bags onto the ground. There were hundreds of maps and papers. But which one was the time chart? They had to find it fast. The Professor could return at any moment.

Can you find the time chart?

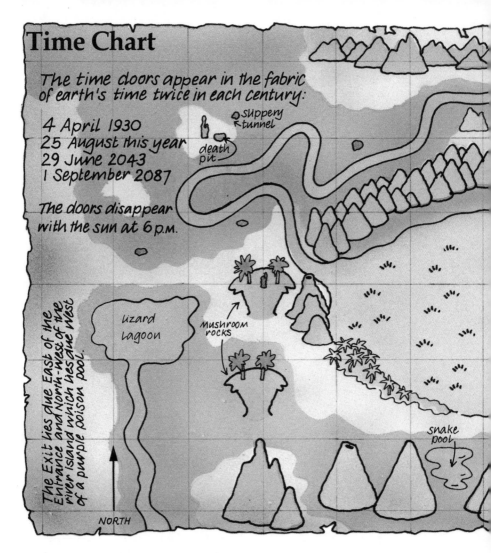

Time Chart

The time doors appear in the fabric of earth's time twice in each century:

4 April 1930
25 August this year
29 June 2043
1 September 2087

The doors disappear with the sun at 6 p.m.

slippery tunnel

death pit

lizard lagoon

mushroom rocks

snake pool

The Exit lies due East of the Entrance and North-West of the river island which lies due West of a purple poison pool.

NORTH

Zack untied the red ribbon and carefully unrolled the tattered, old chart. He spread it out on the ground in front of them.

"It's a map of the whole area," Jo exclaimed. "The Professor must have been here before."

Zack, Jo and Freddie stared blankly at the map. They were stumped. The nest was marked with an arrow. But where was the time door? It wasn't shown anywhere.

"This is hopeless," Freddie wailed. "We'll never find our way home."

There are two time doors, an Entrance and an Exit. Both appear as a hole through which the past or future can be seen.

mushroom rock

pillar rocks

lava pool

crocodile swamp

river islands

swamp island

The Entrance lies due East of the death pit and North-East of the tree stump on the mushroom rock.

purple poison pools

blue-capped volcano

nest

Jo was about to agree when she started reading the strange, spidery notes scrawled at the sides of the map.

"I think these are clues," she explained, pointing at the notes. "If we work out the compass bearings, we can find the time door."

Jo studied the map while Zack and Freddie kept watch.

"I've found it," Jo said.

. . . Just in time. The Professor was returning. Quickly, they dived for cover.

Can you find the time door?

Crocodile Swamp

The Professor stared in horror at the mess. Papers and maps lay everywhere.

"Run for it," Zack yelled, sprinting towards the jungle.

Too late. The Professor spotted them at once and started off in hot pursuit.

Zack, Jo and Freddie ran on and on as fast as they could, until they came to the edge of a vast, steamy swamp.

"We've got to cross this swamp," said Zack. "It's the quickest way to the time door."

"We can use that hollow tree trunk as a canoe," said a voice.

It was Arthur! He had escaped from the Professor. Jo and Freddie scrambled into the trunk, as Zack and Arthur pushed them out into the swamp. But what could they use as paddles?

"We can't use our hands," said Arthur. "Look at those crocodiles!"

He was right. Then Jo realized she and Zack both had something they could use.

What can they use as paddles?

Freddie and the Monstermagus

At the other side, the swamp was surrounded by a wall of steep mountains and volcanoes. There was only one way through – a narrow, muddy pass at the foot of a smoking volcano. A stream of red-hot lava was starting to pour down the side of the volcano towards the pass.

They dashed to the pass, ran under a rocky ledge and on to safety. But where was Freddie? They looked back. He was still a long way off, paddling in the water. And there behind him was . . . a huge Monstermagus.

"What can we do? What's going to happen?" wailed Jo.

Ledge

"It's obvious," said Arthur, tapping his calculator keys.

Zack and Jo looked blank, so Arthur explained.

"The lava is heading for that ledge. Freddie has to run eight metres to pass under its midpoint and he does 100 metres in 25 seconds."

"The lava flows two metres in a second. It's six metres above the ledge which is 17 metres from the ground. The Monstermagus is 16 metres behind Freddie, runs six metres a second and we already know how tall it is."

Can you work out what happens?

Looking for the Time Door

They clambered on up through the pass until they came out into open ground. They could see jungle just a little way ahead. The time door was here somewhere . . .

Freddie stopped shaking and began grumbling.

"I was nearly eaten and it's all your fault, Zack," he muttered. "This expedition was your idea. I was quite happy being bored at home."

But no one was taking any notice. They were running out of time.

Zack unrolled the Professor's chart. There were now only minutes left before the time door disappeared. They HAD to find it.

"We're in the right place," said Zack. "But where's the door?"

"We have to look for it," said Arthur. "It should be easy to see."

They paced up and down searching. Suddenly they spotted it!

Where is the time door?

The Footprint Fossil

Back in their own time, it was hard to believe it had ever happened. Fossilwood Forest was as dark and gloomy as ever and even the Professor looked less crazy.

From behind a bush, they watched as the Professor struggled through the forest with his precious chest. What would he do when he realized it was full of stones? What would he say when he discovered Arthur had taken the film out of his camera?

The next day, they took the Monstermagus claw and a few prehistoric shells to the museum. The first thing they saw was the famous footprints fossil. They gazed at the small human shoeprint.

"You know who made it don't you?" Jo laughed.

"No one would believe us if we tried to explain!" said Zack.

Do you know who made the fossil footprint?

Clues

Pages 102-103
You can see what the claw looks like in Zack's newspaper on page 101.

Pages 104-105
This is easy. First follow Zack's route to find out where it takes them. Then follow Jo's and Freddie's routes in turn.

Pages 106-107
Freddie's dinosaur book on pages 108 and 109 makes this easy.

Pages 110-111
Work out which are Zack, Jo and Freddie's footprints. Are there any others?

Pages 112-113
Trace each piece of paper, or photocopy the page and cut out the pieces. Match them up and stick them together to read the diary.

Pages 114-115
Look back at Zak's newspaper on page 101.

Pages 116-117
What does Freddie have with him? Look at pages 102 and 103.

Pages 118-119
You don't need a clue for this. Use your eyes.

Pages 120-121
Arthur's note on page 108 and Professor Crank-Pott's diary on pages 112 and 113 should give you some hints.

Pages 122-123
This is easy. They can jump from pillar to pillar and climb over the tree.

Pages 124-125
Try exchanging the last letter of the first word with the first letter of the next word.

Pages 126-127
Find the missing numbers first. Ascending means going up.

Pages 128-129
Arthur's note on page 125 describes the time chart.

Pages 130-131
Find the time door entrance first. Remember the points of the compass:

Pages 132-133
What equipment do both Zack and Jo have? Look at pages 102 and 103.

Pages 134-135
Use Arthur's figures to work out how long it will take Freddie, the Monstermagus and the lava to pass the ledge.

Pages 136-137
Can you spot anything unusual in the picture?

Page 138
Look back through the book at everyone's shoeprints.

Answers

Pages 102-103

Here is the Monstermagus claw.

Pages 104-105

This map shows each person's route. Freddie's is the only correct one. Zack's route takes them to the Wild Woods.

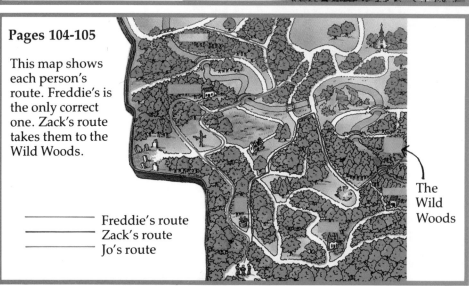

————— Freddie's route
————— Zack's route
————— Jo's route

The Wild Woods

Pages 106-107

Here you can see which dinosaurs eat meat and which eat plants.

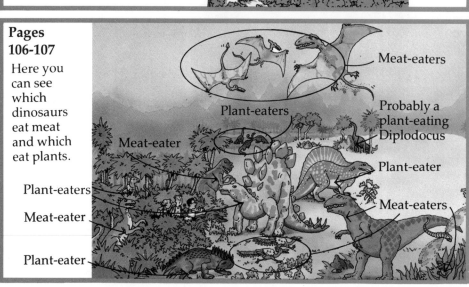

Meat-eaters

Plant-eaters

Probably a plant-eating Diplodocus

Plant-eater

Meat-eaters

Meat-eater

Plant-eaters

Meat-eater

Plant-eater

Jo has seen five different sets of shoeprints. This means two other people have also travelled backwards in time.

These footprints do not belong to Zack, Jo or Freddie.

Freddie's footprint
Zack's footprint
Jo's footprint

Pages 112-113

This is the page from the diary, when the pieces are put together.

> AUGUST
> MONDAY 20th
> All the figures work. At long last I've found the secret of the time door again. Recruited a boy called Arthur as my assistant. He's brilliant at sums, but I don't like children at all.
>
> TUESDAY 21st
> Making plans. The time door appears on Saturday I shall travel back 150 million years and steal some dinosaur eggs. Then I shall bring them home and hatch them I shall cause chaos in the modern world with my little pets
>
> WEDNESDAY 22nd
> Spent the day digging at the dinosaur site in Fossilwood Forest with a lot of silly experts They think I'm mad, but I'll prove them wrong – I'm a genius !
>
> THURSDAY 23rd
> At the site again Gilbert, my pet python, is a little off-colour. Gave him some special potion. Clumsy Arthur dropped my favourite test tube
>
> FRIDAY 24th
> Success ! Fame at last I have found the skeleton of a real monster of a dinosaur and called it Monstermagus. Arthur was late this morning and he overcooked my swordfish steak. He will suffer for it Gilbert is better
>
> SATURDAY 25th
> My plan goes ahead today I shall steal the eggs of the Monstermagus. If my calculations are correct, I will find its nest in a desert clearing near purple poison pools

Pages 114-115

The man is Professor Crank-Pott. Zack recognizes him from the newspaper photo on page 101, shown below.

Pages 116-117
Freddie has an inflatable air cushion (see pages 102 and 103). They can blow it up and cling on to it. This will keep them afloat as the cave floods. When the water reaches the roof, they can scramble out of the hole at the top.

Pages 118-119

Arthur's trail is marked here in black.

Pages 120-121

The nest is behind this volcano. Arthur's note on page 117 says the nest is South of a blue-capped volcano, South of the swamp. The Professor's diary on pages 112 and 113 says it is in a desert clearing near purple poison pools.

South is directly ahead of Zack

Pages 122-123

The route down the rocky pillars is marked in black.

They climb over this tree.

Pages 124-125

The message is decoded by swapping the last letter of every word with the first letter of the next.

You are very near the nest. Don't worry about the Monstermagus. The Professor's dart will put it to sleep for one hour. You can find the time doors on the Professor's time chart – it's an old, torn roll of paper tied with one red ribbon.

Pages 126-127

Here is the box with the missing numbers added. The buttons marked 2, 4, 6 and 8 will open the lock.

Pages 128-129

This is the only one of the papers that fits Arthur's description on page 125.

Pages 130-131

The compass bearings pinpoint the time doors, marked below.

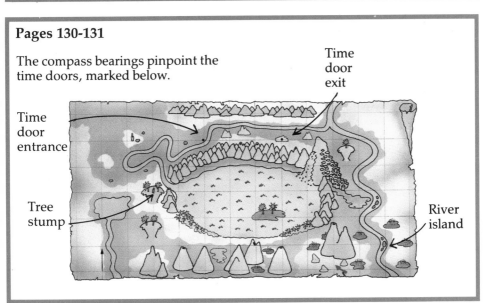

Time door exit

Time door entrance

Tree stump

River island

Pages 132-133

Zack and Jo both have spades which they can use as paddles.

Pages 134-135

Freddie runs four metres a second so he will pass under the ledge in two seconds' time. The lava will reach the ledge, way above him, in three seconds' time, so Freddie is safe.

The Monstermagus will pass under the ledge in four seconds' time. At this point, the lava will be 15 metres from the ground which means it will hit the Monstermagus on the head. The Monstermagus is 15 metres tall (see Zack's newspaper on page 101).

Pages 136-137

Here is the time door.

Through it, you can see St Elmo's Church, shown in the map on pages 104 and 105.

Page 138

Freddie is the only one whose footprint matches the fossil print. The print was made in the soft mud when Freddie was running away from Monstermagus. The volcanic lava preserved his and the dinosaur's footprints, as well as the skeleton. They eventually became fossils (see pages 108-109).

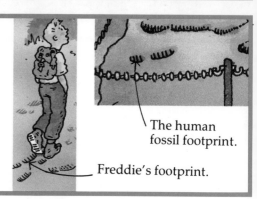

The human fossil footprint.

Freddie's footprint.

ESCAPE FROM
BLOOD CASTLE

Jenny Tyler

Designed and illustrated
by Graham Round

Cover design: Nancy Leschnikoff

Contents

About this Story

Escape from Blood Castle is a strange and exciting adventure. Its hero is Intrepid Ivor. Follow him through the underground maze, on to the roof and down into the dungeons of Blood Castle as he hunts for the all-important Papers.

The story begins over the page. Just start reading. At the bottom of the page, there is a puzzle to solve. Don't turn over until you have found the answer. If you get stuck, there are extra clues on page 185. You will find all the answers on pages 186 to 192.

COUSIN BORIS

INTREPID IVOR

THE FRIENDLY SPIDER

THE MOUSE WHO HELPS IVOR

Intrepid Ivor and the Evil Baron

Ivor's heart thumped as he crouched, shivering, among the bushes. Looming in front of him was the object of his thoughts for many months – Blood Castle, home of the man Ivor knew as Cousin Boris, but who now refused to answer to anything but The Baron. Perhaps he should just turn round now and run home.

Ivor thought of his favourite TV heroes and pulled himself together. He couldn't let himself be cheated of wealth and title by his creepy cousin. His friends would never call him Intrepid Ivor again if he funked this.

Pausing only to check he still had his trusty survival kit in his pockets (useful things, such as chewing gum, pepper, nylon thread and half a chocolate bar), Intrepid Ivor made his way towards the castle's west wall, darting stealthily from bush to bush.

How to get in was the first problem. Ivor thoughtfully sucked his finger where it had caught on the sharp hook in his pocket and surveyed the scene in front of him. Suddenly he worked out what to do . . .

DON'T TURN THE PAGE YET.

This picture shows the building as Ivor saw it. How and where did Ivor get in?

GARGOYLES

SHARP SPIKES

POISONOUS LEAVES

YESTERDAY'S MILK

148

Inside Blood Castle

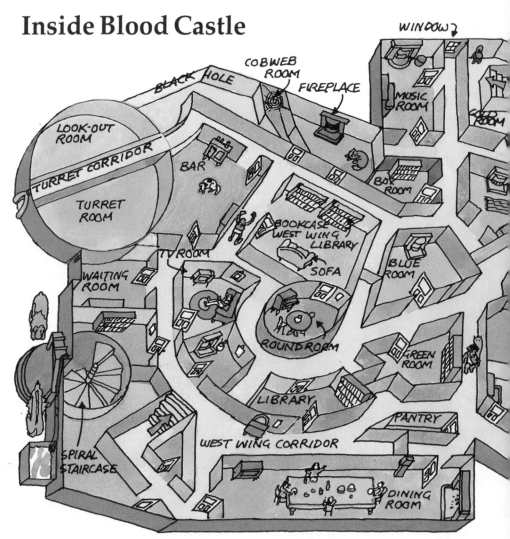

It was pitch black inside. Ivor shuffled along, feeling his way along the wall with his hand. He could see nothing – it was like walking blindfold. His ears strained for the slightest sound, but there was none.

He felt the corridor curve to the left and then turn sharp right. For a short distance the surface beneath his fingers became very smooth, but soon changed again to the same roughish texture as before. A dozen or so steps further on he felt the same temporary smoothness beneath his fingertips again. For the first time he could hear something. He paused. A faint snoring sort of sound reached his ears. He crept onwards – a slight left turn, followed by quite a sharp one and then a shaft of light.

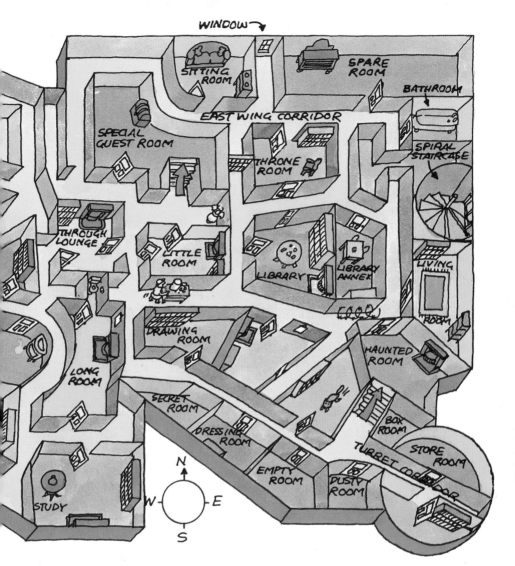

At last he could have a look at the map in his pocket and try to work out where he was.

Ivor's intention was to find the ital Papers which would show who was the rightful heir to Blood Castle. He had been told that they were in a oom with two doors on adjacent valls and a fireplace on the wall

opposite the larger door, with a large bookcase to its left.

DON'T TURN THE PAGE YET.

Above is a copy of the map Ivor carried in his pocket.
Where is Ivor now?
Which room should he go to and which route should he take to get there?

The Locked Door

BELL PULL

MATILDA

UNCLE SPIKE'S WALKING STICKS

COAL BUCKET

FELIX

COLD TEA

With shaking hand, Ivor edged the door open. Yes, there was the fireplace facing him with a bookcase to its left. It must be the right room. He opened the door a little wider and crept in.

A few steps took him to the middle of the room. Then his heart stopped as he heard a loud bang behind him, followed by the unmistakable sound of a key turning slowly in a rusty lock. He rushed to the door in a panic. It was indeed locked. The other door! Of course that was locked too.

As he frantically searched the room for a way out, Ivor almost forgot why he was there in the first place. The Papers! He might as well use his energy looking for them.

Nothing. In despair, Ivor sank down next to the bookcase and stared at the books.

"You've made a mess of this, Ivor," he thought to himself.

Suddenly he realized there was something very odd about the books. Picking a scrap of paper out of the waste-paper basket, he started scribbling furiously.

"Got it!" he said aloud and jumped to his feet. In a few seconds he was out of the room.

DON'T TURN THE PAGE YET.

What did Ivor see and how did he get out of the room?

153

Another Map?

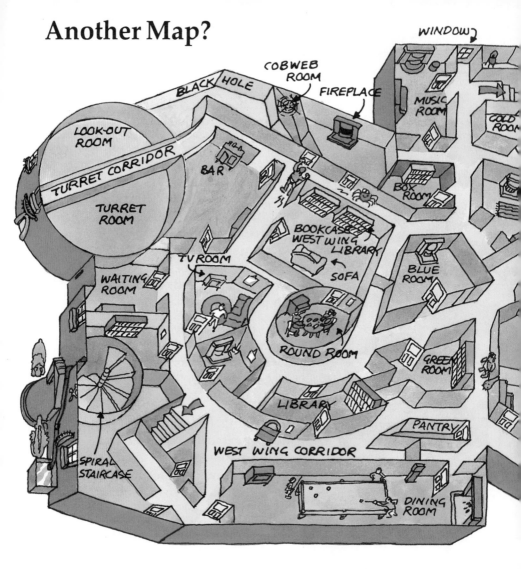

I vor found himself in another room. He tried the door straight away. Whew! It wasn't locked.

He leaned against it, breathing a sigh of relief and realized, as he did so, that he still had in his hand the screwed-up scrap of paper he had been scribbling on. He was about to toss it away when he saw

it had something on the back. He smoothed it out on the table and found that it was a map. It looked just like the one he had in his pocket. But was it really the same?

It took a minute or two for Ivor to check his heavily laden pockets, but eventually he found his own map, neatly folded up.

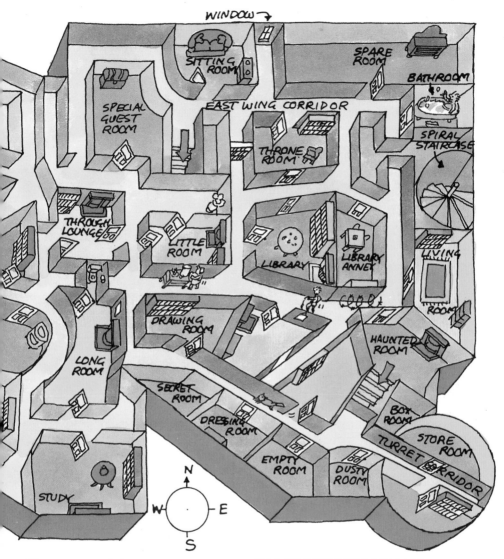

He compared the two maps very carefully. There were lots of tiny differences. Suddenly Ivor knew why he hadn't found the Papers – he'd been in the wrong room all the time. What's more, he knew what he had to do next.

Quickly snatching a useful-looking box from the table, he set off.

DON'T TURN THE PAGE.

This is the map Ivor found. Compare it with the one he had in his pocket (on pages 6-7) and see if you can find all the differences. How did Ivor know he'd been in the wrong room?

Where did he set off to?

Ivor Meets the Tea Trolley

Feeling rather pleased with himself, Ivor quickly made his way to the stairs.

The noise was a shock. In his haste, he had forgotten that danger could be lurking round every corner. He thought it sounded a bit like crockery rattling, but decided he was being silly. It was obviously something much more sinister. It was getting louder too.

Suddenly all was quiet again. A friendly looking spider scuttled across the floor in front of him. Ivor enticed it into the little box he had in his hand. It made him feel better to have a friend – even if it was only a spider.

After waiting for what seemed like ages, Ivor spread himself round the corner at the top of the stairs. He was in an empty room. As he tip-toed out of the door and into the corridor, he could smell something which reminded him of strong, well-brewed tea.

Ivor crept along the corridors until eventually he spotted the source of the smell. There, all alone, was a tea trolley. A huge urn steamed gently among piles of the most delicious looking cakes and buns.

ARTHUR

FE

PEARL'S FAVOURITE DRINK

SPIDER HOLE

GRANDFATHER BLOOD'S ARABIAN VASE

Ivor couldn't resist cakes and there didn't seem to be anyone about . . .
DON'T TURN THE PAGE YET.

Ivor strained his eyes and just managed to read the notice propped up on the tea trolley. We've magnified it so you can read it. Which cakes can Ivor eat safely?

The Family

AUNT MATILDA

TALL & THIN

LIKES CROCODILES & CATS (NOT MUCH ELSE)

GREY HAIR

OFTEN READS STORIES TO HER CROCODILES

COUSIN HERBERT

SHORT-SIGHTED

SCAR

PODGY

HORACE'S TWIN BROTHER

LIMPS BUT CHANGES LEG SOMETIMES

I vor picked the stickiest looking cake and bit into it. The red jam ran down his chin. "Yum yum, terrif...", he thought, then something seemed to go wrong with his brain. The Tea lady's hideously ugly face loomed very close to his own. The ground seemed closer than it should be too . . .

The bumping, banging and rattling was making his head ache and he felt sick, but luckily the brain disease seemed to have gone away. He cautiously moved his body and found he was sitting on the tea trolley. His feet and hands were roped to the four corners of it.

A strangled grunt and a violent jolt of the trolley prompted Ivor to peer cautiously out, but all he could see

AWFUL ARTHUR

WIRY HAIR

RELATIONSHIP UNKNOWN

KEEN DIVER

TEETH

CLUMSY

PLAYS SAXOPHONE BADLY

NEPHEW NORMAN

TALL

CHOCOLATE TOFFEE

GLASSES

SPOTS

ANOTHER CHOCOLATE TOFFEE

LIKES TV AND COMPUTER GAMES

was a frightened spider, the twin of his friend in the box, scurrying down the corridor.

He stared again at the Tea Lady. Could she be one of Boris's "family" in disguise? He thought about some photographs he had once seen of them.

A sudden awful stomach-lurch

told him they were in a lift – going down. "That's the one!" thought Ivor, just as his stomach settled in its right place again and the lift doors opened. "That might be useful", he thought and dozed off again.

DON'T TURN THE PAGE YET.

Here are the photographs of the family which Ivor had seen. Which of them do you think is the tea lady?

Captured!

CHANDELIER

COGS

MOUSE

PENDULUM

CHEESE SANDWICH

BOX

LEVER

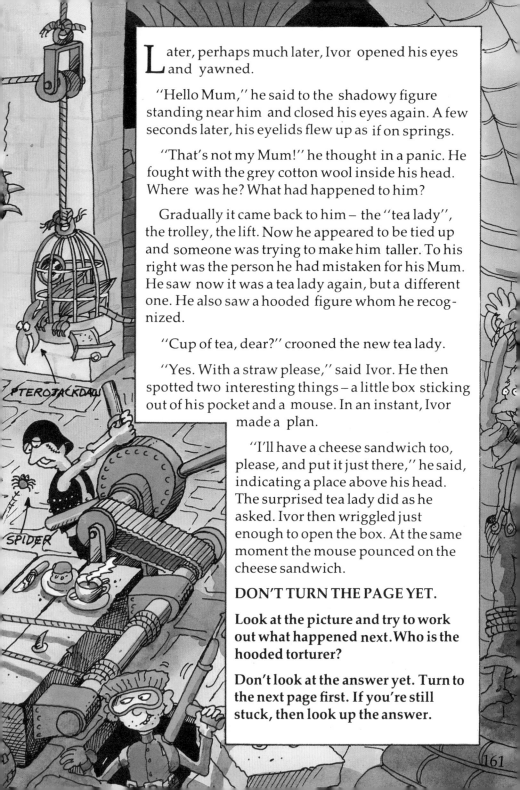

Later, perhaps much later, Ivor opened his eyes and yawned.

"Hello Mum," he said to the shadowy figure standing near him and closed his eyes again. A few seconds later, his eyelids flew up as if on springs.

"That's not my Mum!" he thought in a panic. He fought with the grey cotton wool inside his head. Where was he? What had happened to him?

Gradually it came back to him – the "tea lady", the trolley, the lift. Now he appeared to be tied up and someone was trying to make him taller. To his right was the person he had mistaken for his Mum. He saw now it was a tea lady again, but a different one. He also saw a hooded figure whom he recognized.

"Cup of tea, dear?" crooned the new tea lady.

"Yes. With a straw please," said Ivor. He then spotted two interesting things – a little box sticking out of his pocket and a mouse. In an instant, Ivor made a plan.

"I'll have a cheese sandwich too, please, and put it just there," he said, indicating a place above his head. The surprised tea lady did as he asked. Ivor then wriggled just enough to open the box. At the same moment the mouse pounced on the cheese sandwich.

DON'T TURN THE PAGE YET.

Look at the picture and try to work out what happened next. Who is the hooded torturer?

Don't look at the answer yet. Turn to the next page first. If you're still stuck, then look up the answer.

PTEROJACKDAW

SPIDER

What Really Happened?

These pictures show what happened in the dungeon during the chaos that followed the spider's escape – or do they?

Some of these things happened, but not in the order shown. Can you sort out which pictures tell the truth and in what order?

The lever pulls the trapdoor open, letting the balls through.

The mouse jumps on Roxanne's nose and she runs away.

The mouse jumps on to the sandwich, pushing the lever down.

The pterojackdaw's cage falls on Horace's head and knocks him out.

The pterojackdaw gets free and attacks Arthur.

The noose tightens round Roxanne's foot, tripping her up and knocking over the tea trolley.

The rope holding the pendulum burns and it crashes down.

8 Ivor wriggles up the bed and is able to unhook his handropes.

9 Arthur is submerged by the contents of the tea trolley.

10 The spider frightens Horace who lets go of the wheel, loosening Ivor's ropes.

11 The chandelier is winched up by the machine and the candles burn through the rope holding the cage.

Ivor adds to his "useful" things

The dungeon floor was littered with bits and pieces. Ivor couldn't resist cramming some of them into his already overloaded pockets. Here you can see what he picked up.

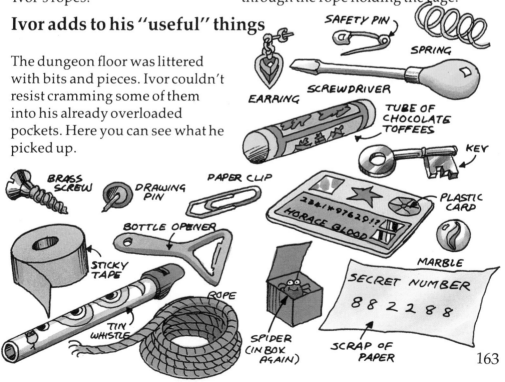

SAFETY PIN

SPRING

SCREWDRIVER

EARRING

TUBE OF CHOCOLATE TOFFEES

KEY

BRASS SCREW

DRAWING PIN

PAPER CLIP

234/*97629!?

HORACE GLOOD

PLASTIC CARD

STICKY TAPE

BOTTLE OPENER

MARBLE

SECRET NUMBER 882288

TIN WHISTLE

ROPE

SPIDER (IN BOX AGAIN)

SCRAP OF PAPER

163

Escape from the Dungeon

GRANDFATHER BLOOD'S BICYCLE

ROXANNE'S MUMMY

USED TO CONTAIN A PLANT

FRUIT MACHINE

HORACE'S DISGUISE

SPIDER-EATING PLANT

PEARL'S BICYCLE

THE MOUSE THAT HELPED IVOR ESCAPE

SLIME

Ivor grabbed a sandwich from the overturned tea trolley and, with pockets and cheeks bulging, he thought about what to next.

Obviously he must get out of the dungeon before Horace and the others came to. Then he must find the lift and the Papers. But which of the seven identical green doors should he go through?

He had been half-asleep, half-awake while the tea trolley had trundled him along. Hazy memories floated into his mind. Yes, he

AWFUL ARTHUR'S PRIZE PIRANHA

HORACE'S FRIENDS

BORIS

POISONOUS PALM

NORMAN'S BICYCLE

BLOOD FAMILY COAT OF ARMS

ARTHUR'S BICYCLE

5

6

7

FRUIT MACHINE

MORE OF PEARL'S EMPTIES

STINGING FERN

FRUIT MACHINE

PEARL'S EMPTIES

TO THE SEWER

UNCLE SPIKE'S LOST ROLLER SKATE

remembered entering the dungeon now. He had passed close to a fruit machine. It was on his left . . . or was it right? He remembered the trolley's back right-hand wheel brushing past a bicycle and almost knocking it over, too. He concentrated harder and remembered something odd

hanging from the ceiling and some crates in front of the fruit machine.

DON'T TURN THE PAGE YET.

Which of the doors in the picture should Ivor go through?

Norman and the Pinball Machine

Having made his decision, Ivor pushed the door. It wouldn't open. He pushed again, leaning his whole weight on it, and suddenly it swung open. He stumbled through into the gloom and found himself face to chest with nephew Norman.

"Hello," said Norman. "Who are you? Come and play pinball with me."

Ivor gulped and produced what he hoped was a friendly smile. He'd never come higher than 153rd on the school pinball ladder. Norman's vice-like grip on his arm didn't encourage him to refuse and he found himself being led along the corridor.

After two left and three right turns, Norman opened a door.

"Wow!" said Ivor. The most amazing pinball machine Ivor had ever seen stood in the middle of the room. It was huge and covered with brightly coloured pictures and lights.

"My turn first," said Norman, who immediately sent the first ball whizzing round the machine. Ivor's eyes grew bigger and rounder as he watched. This boy was GOOD. He notched up a score of 208,361 with one ball!

"OK", said Norman, "now you've got to match my score exactly, or I shan't let you leave the room."

DON'T TURN THE PAGE YET.

What route should Ivor's ball take round the machine to match Norman's score?

TOP SCORER: G. BLOOD

208,361

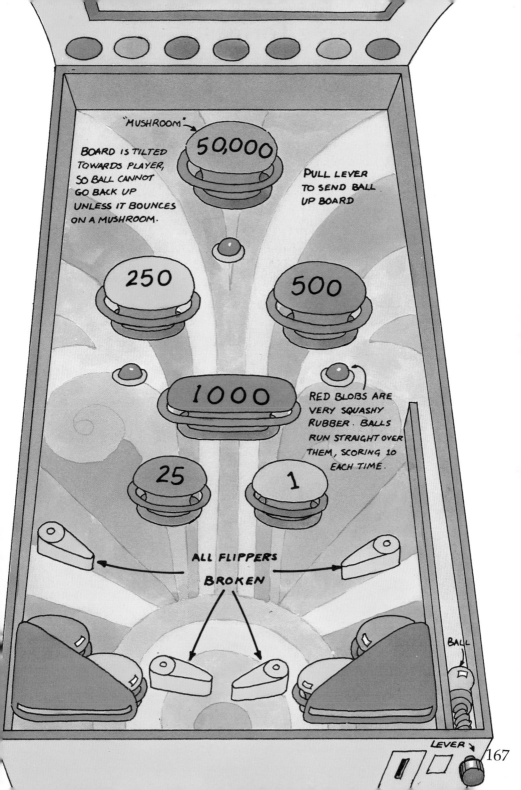

"MUSHROOM"

BOARD IS TILTED
TOWARDS PLAYER,
SO BALL CANNOT
GO BACK UP
UNLESS IT BOUNCES
ON A MUSHROOM.

50,000

PULL LEVER
TO SEND BALL
UP BOARD

250

500

1000

RED BLOBS ARE
VERY SQUASHY
RUBBER. BALLS
RUN STRAIGHT OVER
THEM, SCORING 10
EACH TIME.

25

1

ALL FLIPPERS
BROKEN

BALL

LEVER

167

The Surprising Toffees

Norman jumped up and down hysterically. "3325! You'll have to stay here for ever!"

Ivor's heart couldn't sink any further. He reached into his pocket and pulled out the tube of chocolate toffees he'd found in the torture room.

"Want one?" he said, and Norman's greedy eyes lit up. He took ten and crammed them all in his mouth at once. Disgusted, Ivor took one for himself and was on the point of putting it in his mouth, when he noticed Norman's face change. He made a strangled sound and crashed heavily to the floor.

Horrified, Ivor dropped the toffee he was holding and let the rest of the packet fall after it.

He turned to go but the walls were completely covered with shelves. There was no sign of the door. He scanned the room, searching for a clue to the way out. The cursor on the computer screen winked at him.

"Which way?" it asked. Ivor felt like kicking it. He pressed some keys and got a picture on the screen.

"Oh, I see," he said.

DON'T TURN THE PAGE YET.

What did Ivor do next?

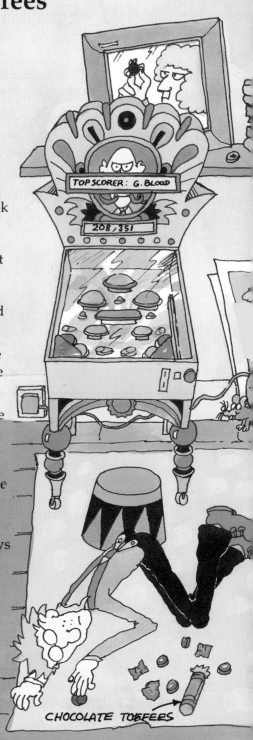

CHOCOLATE TOFFEES

Blood Castle Underground

Ivor squeezed through the hole and found himself in a twisty passage. Somehow or other he must find his way to the lift and get back upstairs. **DON'T TURN THE PAGE YET.**

Work out where Ivor is and which route he should take to the lift.

(NOTE: SOME OF THE PASSAGES GO BEHIND OTHERS — YOU ARE ALLOWED TO GO ALONG THESE.)

PORTRAITS OF BORIS CONCEAL TV CAMERAS — AVOID THEM.

AWFUL ARTHUR'S PRACTICE TANK

SHARK

BORIS →

NEPHEW NORMAN

TRAP DOOR

TRAP- DOOR IN FLOOR

BORIS

SLIPPERY SHAFT

SHARP SPIKES

PAULINE

PEARL'S HIDE AWAY

ROXANNE'S MAKE-UP ROOM

SNAKE PIT

WAY OUT

BORIS →

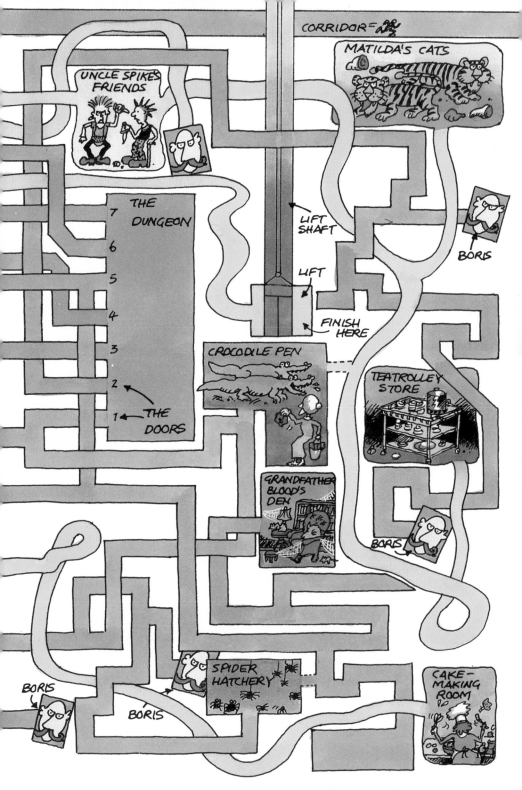

At last Ivor found himself standing in front of a lift. He stepped inside and the door closed behind him. The control panel looked like an aeroplane flight deck and was so high up Ivor had to stand on tip-toe to see it. There were flashing coloured lights, digital displays, dials and gauges, and a set of buttons numbered from zero to nine. Ivor did some calculations and decided which button to press.

Nothing happened. On closer examination, he realized that the buttons were shielded by a layer of clear perspex.

SPIKE

Ivor stared thoughtfully at the panel. He then started poking at it with something he found in his pocket. Ah! Something was happening. The perspex panel slid across to expose the buttons, so Ivor pressed some of them and, at last, the lift set off upwards.

A voice in his ear made Ivor jump higher than the control panel. It seemed to be coming from the portrait of Boris hanging on the wall.

"He's escaped. Guard the East Turret immediately. Repeat. Guard the East Turret."

"Gosh," thought Ivor, "They must think I'm Horace!"

The lift stopped as suddenly as it had started, the doors slid open and Ivor stepped out.

DON'T TURN THE PAGE YET.

How did Ivor make the lift work and why did "they" think he was Horace?

On the Roof

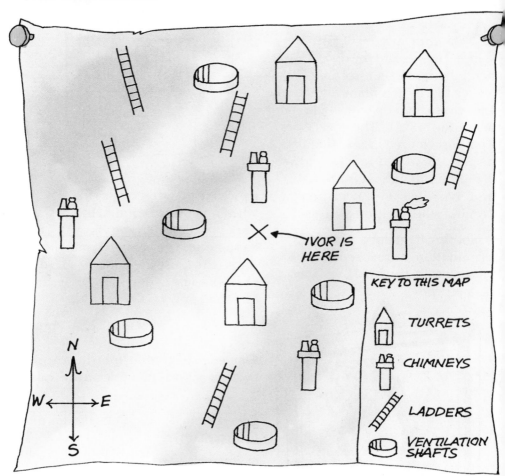

KEY TO THIS MAP

TURRETS

CHIMNEYS

LADDERS

VENTILATION SHAFTS

IVOR IS HERE

N
W → E
S

A cold wind hit Ivor in the face. He was outdoors! He walked to the nearest wall, leaned over and pulled sharply back. He was an awfully long way from the ground.

Ivor threaded his way through the ventilation shafts and chimneys. He was wondering where to go next when he came across a map.

"If they are so keen on guarding the east turret," he thought, "there must be something of interest there. It must be that one . . . or that one. Hmmm, which direction is east?"

DON'T TURN THE PAGE YET.

Above you can see the map Ivor is looking at and, on the right, the roofscape views (not in order) he sees by turning through 90° at a time. What is the colour of the door on the east turret?

174

175

What the Papers Say

Ivor kicked open the brightly painted door like people do in gangster films and waited to see what would happen.

"Stick 'em up!" screamed a harsh voice and Ivor did so, terrified.

"Stick 'em up! Steeck 'emm uppp! Steeeeeck 'emmmmmmmmmm uppppppppppppppppppp! Whirr clank."

Ivor pushed the door again. Silence. There was no-one in sight. He went in, almost tripping over an ancient tape recorder and the deep carpet. Expensive-looking paintings hung on the walls. There was certainly something of interest here. He glanced through an open door and saw a sumptuously furnished office, complete with antique desk.

The room was empty, so Ivor tip-

TESTAMENT

OKER TABLE, MY
VER SAFETY PINS
Y SON SPIKE, MY
MY DIVING
ON TO ART

ANTIQUE SIL
BOXES TO MY
LEG TO HERBER
HARPOON COLLECTI
HA BIRD AND MY
TO BABY NORMAN
F 'THE CROCODILE' AN
Y, TO MATILDA AN
STREI

THIS IS
OF GRA
I HEREB
COLLECTION
AND MY JUKE
WOODEN
GEAR AND
MY PIRAN
MACHINE
COPIES O
MONTHL
ENT

toed in. Perhaps the Papers would be here – they would surely have been moved from their original hiding place by now. He searched the desk drawers but found nothing. He glanced around the room but all he could see was a very dirty, dog-eared envelope which had fallen on the floor. He picked it up and looked inside. All it contained was torn scraps of paper. He tipped them out on to the desk, idly wondering what they could be.

Then a few words caught his eye: "Last will . . . Blood . . . wealth . . . ." and he frantically started putting together this paper jigsaw puzzle.

DON'T TURN THE PAGE YET.

What do the scraps of paper say?

(HER TO
AND MY HOME KNOWN
CASTLE, ALL MY WORLDLY
MY EXOTIC SNAKE COLLEC
TO MY GRANDSON BORIS
PATE

PINBALL
THE BOUND
PEARL, MY
THE LOCAL HOSPITAL
TO ALL AS BLOOD
WEALTH AND
CTION
'SPIDER KEEPER'S
ND 'SPIDER KEEPER'S
HUR,

THE WILL
THE LAST WILL AND
ND FATHER BLOOD
Y LEAVE MY SNO
OF

Ivor Meets Boris

Ivor's brain hurt . . . and his heart too. This wasn't what he'd expected to find! He stuffed the scraps back into the envelope, pushed it into his pocket and turned to leave the room.

There, outlined in the doorway, was Boris.

Ivor wasn't even scared any more. He was too disheartened to care what happened next. He stared coolly at the tall, still figure.

What did happen next surprised him. He heard his own voice cry out.

"You're not Boris!" it said.

DON'T TURN THE PAGE YET.

How did Ivor know that the man in front of him was not Boris?

BORIS: A STUDY OF HANDS

MY EAR BY ARTHUR

ROXANNE

THE DESK

THE TWINS AT PLAY

The Prisoner

Ivor darted for the door and slipped past Boris's legs before Boris had time to close his mouth. Down the corridor, up some steps and through a door sped Ivor. He waited breathing heavily. There was no sign that he had been followed.

The room was very gloomy.

BORIS
BY
MATILDA

He could hardly see anything at all, but he could hear some faint sounds coming from somewhere to his left. He found a door. The noises were definitely coming from the other side of it.

The door was stiff and creaky but there was more light on the other side. Ivor couldn't believe his eyes. There, inside a gigantic cage, was Boris! A few seconds' thought led Ivor to the conclusion that it must be the real Boris, his genuine cousin.

"Ivor! How pleased I am to see you!" said Boris.

Ivor didn't reply. He was still suspicious of Boris, real or not.

"I've been a prisoner here since Grandfather Blood died and Wicked Wilf came back from Australia and started impersonating me. You've got to help me to escape."

"OK," Ivor said, after a while. "I've got an idea. Hand me that rope."

Ivor then proceeded to free Boris from his cage.

DON'T TURN THE PAGE YET.

What did Ivor do to release Boris from the cage?

The Escape Plan

A scrap of paper on the floor caught Ivor's eye. He picked it up. This is it:

GRANDSON IVOR, PROVIDING MY DAUGHTER MATILDA IS STILL ALIVE AND MY

"What's that?" asked Boris. Ivor showed him and the rest of the pieces he'd found in the envelope.

"The Will! We've no time to lose! We must find Aunt Matilda and get out of Blood Castle as soon as possible, so we can claim our inheritances. I bet I can guess where she'll be and, what's more, I know how we can escape!"

"How?" said Ivor, disbelievingly.

"Easy! Grandfather Blood gave me this just before he died. Thank goodness I can read music! You must have seen Aunt Matilda somewhere in the castle. Think carefully."

DON'T TURN THE PAGE YET.

This is what Grandfather Blood gave Boris. How can they use it to help them escape? (You don't have to be able to read music to work it out.) Where did they find Aunt Matilda?

The Truth at Last

Boris's plan worked like a charm. Aunt Matilda was where Ivor had seen her earlier and the three of them made their escape, using Grandfather Blood's music and Ivor's tin whistle.

As they stood outside breathing the fresh air, Ivor realized they were not a stone's throw from where he had started, goodness knows how long ago. Quickly and quietly they made their way through the gate and up the tree-lined road beyond it. When they reached the top of the hill, they paused to look back. They saw the dim shapes of "Boris", Herbert and Horace loading suitcases into Grandfather Blood's battered old Rolls Royce.

"They're running away!" cried Ivor.

"Let them", said Boris. "They won't get far."

They watched while the ancient Rolls chugged through the gate and out of sight. An hour later, tired and breathless, they reached the home of Mr Sprog, the Blood family's lawyer.

Mrs Sprog produced a wonderful tea for them, which they attacked gratefully while they told Mr Sprog their story. After a while, Ivor looked at Boris thoughtfully and said, "I don't understand how you came to have the scrap of the Will which mentioned me."

Boris explained that Wicked Wilf had torn this piece off himself and that he, Boris, had managed to hide it and keep it safe.

"But", said Boris, "What I don't understand is what would have happened to the legacy if Aunt Matilda were not still alive?"

They all looked at Aunt Matilda, who had turned slightly pink.

"Oh well", she said, and produced a scrap of paper from her handbag. This is what it said:

" . . . otherwise everything is to go to World Spider Sanctuary."

She explained her worry that Pearl's passion for spiders might make her do something dangerous.

"Well, there's only one question left," said Mr Sprog. "Who tore up the Will?"

They all looked blankly at each other.

Do you know?

184

Clues

Page 148

Ivor enters in the normal way. He needs something first though. Search the picture carefully for the key to the problem and then work out how he gets hold of it. Beware the SNAKE PIT.

Page 150

Start at the door in the turret in the top left hand corner of the map. Ivor feels his way with his left hand. Smooth areas are doors.

Page 152

Ivor saw the titles were in code. He decoded the title of a large book and found it to be "Snake Charming for Beginners" Try decoding the others.

Page 154

There are at least 23 differences. The most important ones concern the stairs.

Page 156

Trace each piece of paper, or photocopy the page and cut out the pieces. Match them up and stick them together to read the diary.

Page 158

The "tea lady" need not be female. Look for tell tale strands under the wig.

Page 160

The "tea lady" did a quick change. The mouse is quite heavy. What does the lever do?

Page 162

There are 3 false pictures. The rest are true.

Page 164

This one's easy - you don't need a clue!

Page 166

Start by bouncing the ball from 50000 to 500 and back three times.

Page 168

The picture on the screen corresponds to the floor of the room. Ivor thought the second largest rectangle might be the rug.

Page 170

The maze is quite easy. But if you take a wrong route, don't worry. You might see something that comes in useful later on.

Page 172

Look at the things Ivor picked up in the torture room (see page 163). He used two of these.

Page 174

The smoke gives it away.

Page 176

You could trace or photocopy these pieces, cut them out and stick them together to read them.

Page 178

There are portraits of Boris all through the book. Compare them with the figure in the doorway.

Page 180

Notice the pulley in the ceiling, the greasy ring in the top of the cage, the hook on the rope and the ladder.

Page 182

Look on pages 170-171 for Aunt Matilda and a way out. To escape they need one of the things Ivor found on page 163 and Grandfather Blood's Little tune. One of the books on page 152 might be useful too.

Page 184

Look at the portraits throughout the book. They're not all of Boris. Maybe they're not all portraits either.

Answers

Pages 148-149

Ivor notices a key on the window ledge. He climbs up by the route shown and sits on the ledge above the window. He uses the nylon thread and sharp hook from his pocket to make a fishing line and "fishes" for the key. He then climbs down by the same route, unlocks the front door and goes in.

(Did you think you could go in through the open door? This isn't a good idea – the backwards writing on this door says "SNAKE PIT".)

Ivor sits here to fish for key.

Key

Ivor climbs up this way.

Pages 150-151

Here you can see the route Ivor takes and the room he goes to.

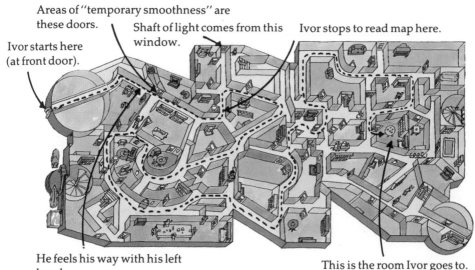

Areas of "temporary smoothness" are these doors.

Shaft of light comes from this window.

Ivor stops to read map here.

Ivor starts here (at front door).

He feels his way with his left hand.

This is the room Ivor goes to.

Pages
152-153

The book titles are all written backwards. The second book from the right on the bottom shelf reads "HANDLE PULL HERE". He pulls it and the bookcase opens revealing the room beyond. (Try decoding the other titles – they may give you some ideas about things that happen later.)

Pages 154-155

Ivor spots that the arrows on the stairs go in different directions and that the new map shows more of the west outside wall. He concludes that his map shows the wrong floor and he needs to search the equivalent room upstairs. He makes for the nearest stairs following the route shown*. Did you find all the other differences too? They are ringed here.

Ivor starts in this room (downstairs).

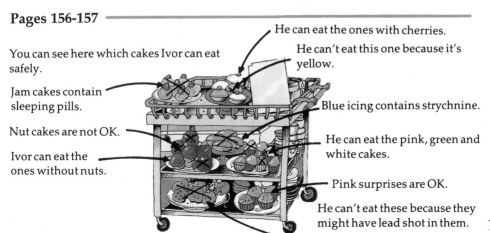

*Ivor is, of course, still on the ground floor. We have shown the route here on the first floor map, but the route on the ground floor is exactly the same.

He takes this route.

He comes up these stairs.

Pages 156-157

You can see here which cakes Ivor can eat safely.

He can eat the ones with cherries.

He can't eat this one because it's yellow.

Jam cakes contain sleeping pills.

Blue icing contains strychnine.

Nut cakes are not OK.

He can eat the pink, green and white cakes.

Ivor can eat the ones without nuts.

Pink surprises are OK.

He can't eat these because they might have lead shot in them.

The "tea lady" is Horace. The strands of red hair give him away. The Pearl "look-alike" wig hides his scar.

Here you can see what happens in the dungeon. The hooded torturer is Horace. His scar is the clue.

Ivor kicks his legs to pull the ropes looser. He can then shift his body far enough up the bed to unhook his hand ropes.

Pendulum winds down, but Ivor is able to escape before it reaches him.

Chandelier goes up.

Candles burn through rope.

Arrows show which way cogs turn.

Cage falls on Horace's head, knocking him out.

Balls turn wheel.

Spider frightens Horace*, who lets go of wheel.

Mouse jumps on to sandwich.

Lever goes down.

This door opens.

This rope tightens round Roxanne's leg

and trips her up. She knocks the tea trolley over.

The cakes and so on fall on Arthur.

Ivor's ropes are loosened when Horace lets go of wheel.

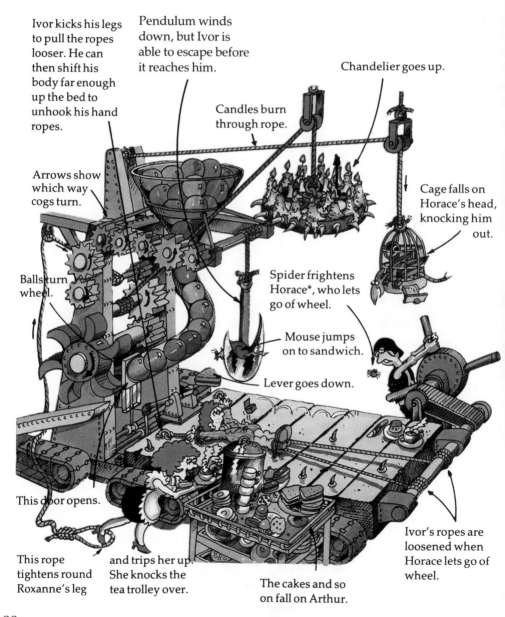

*You know Horace is frightened of spiders from page 159.

Pages 162-163

The pictures go in this order: 3, 10, 1, 6, 11, 4, 9, 8.
Pictures 2, 5 and 7 did not happen. The pendulum comes
down (follow the cogs round to see why) but Ivor has
already escaped.

Pages 164-165

The only door which fits the description completely is door 5.

Pages 166-167

This is the route Norman's ball took.

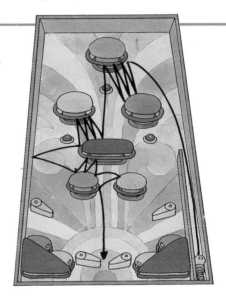

Pages 168-169

Ivor spots that Nephew Norman has a book
on computer games. When he sees the
question "WHICH WAY" on the screen, he
decides to try typing in directions, as you
would if playing a computer adventure
game. When he types "DOWN", a diagram
comes up on the screen. Ivor realizes that
this corresponds to a floor plan of the room
he is in.

Ivor then lifts the rug and finds the
trapdoor, which he opens by pulling the
ring.

(Perhaps you can work out the route
Ivor's ball took on the pinball machine.)

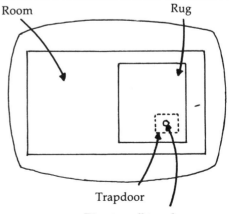

Room

Rug

Trapdoor

Ring to pull trapdoor open.

—— Ivor's route from the dungeon to Norman's room.

- - - Ivor follows this route from Norman's room to the lift.

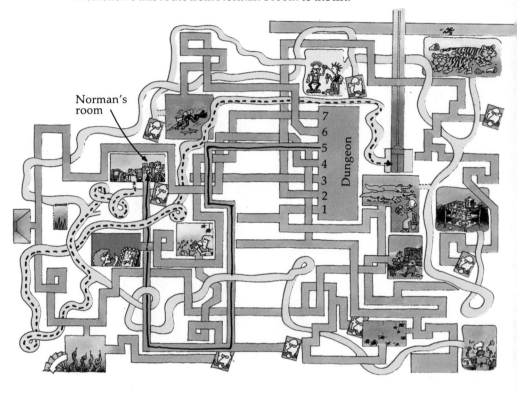

Norman's room

Dungeon

7
6
5
4
3
2
1

Ivor puts the "credit card" he found in the dungeon (see page 163) into the slot and presses the numbers written on the scrap of paper he found with it. This makes the lift work. "They" think he is Horace because the card is in Horace's name.

The east turret door is blue. (If you turn the page round so you can look at the map in the direction of east, you will see the view more clearly.)

Here is the pieced together Will:

THE WILL

THIS IS THE LAST WILL AND TESTAMENT
OF GRANDFATHER BLOOD
I HEREBY LEAVE MY SNOOKER TABLE, MY
COLLECTION OF ANTIQUE SILVER SAFETY PINS
AND MY JUKE BOXES TO MY SON SPIKE, MY
WOODEN LEG TO HERBERT, MY DIVING
GEAR AND HARPOON COLLECTION TO ARTHUR,
MY PIRANHA BIRD AND MY PINBALL
MACHINE TO BABY NORMAN, THE BOUND
COPIES OF 'THE CROCODILE' AND 'SPIDER KEEPER'S
MONTHLY' TO MATILDA AND PEARL, MY
PATENT STRETCHER TO THE LOCAL HOSPITAL
AND MY HOME KNOWN TO ALL AS BLOOD
CASTLE, ALL MY WORLDLY WEALTH AND
MY EXOTIC SNAKE COLLECTION
TO MY GRANDSON BORIS

Ivor had seen several portraits of Boris on his travels through the castle, including one in the room he is now standing in. He notices a number of differences between these and the phoney Boris standing in the doorway. The differences are ringed on this picture.

Ivor props the ladder up against the beam, threads the rope over the pulley and hooks it on to the ring of the cage. He then threads the rope through the ring again and back over the pulley. He then climbs down and pulls on the rope.

The greasiness of the ring helps to reduce the friction between it and the rope. He is just able to pull the cage up enough for Boris to crawl out. He could have threaded the rope through the ring and over the pulley a third time. In theory this would have made the cage easier to lift. However, he was worried about there being too much friction caused by the rope rubbing against itself.

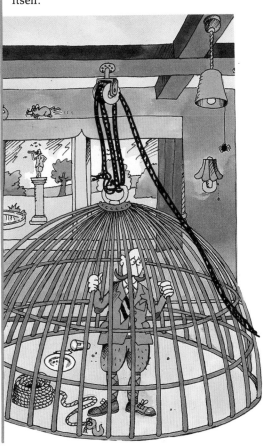

Ivor spotted Aunt Matilda with the crocodiles while he was looking for the lift (see page 171). He and Boris go back there to find her. (Ivor still has the card and number for operating the lift.)

They then make their way to the snake pit. They use the tin whistle Ivor found in the dungeon (page 163) to play Grandfather Blood's Little Tune to charm the snakes so they can get past them safely. (Clues to this are the pictures on the music, Boris's picture "thoughts" on page 182 and the book on "Snake Charming for Beginners" on page 152.) Ivor remembers seeing the snake pit entrance when he was standing outside the castle trying to get in (pages 148-149).

Page 184

On page 157 there is a picture of Uncle Spike on the wall, tearing up some paper. If you look carefully, you will see the words on it are "The Will" in mirror writing, i.e. it is not a portrait, but a reflection in a mirror. So Uncle Spike tore up the Will.

You are probably wondering why. Well, not realizing Boris was an imposter and disgusted by his behaviour after Grandfather Blood's death, Spike thought he would destroy the Will and then try to get rid of Boris. However, you were not the only one to see him doing it. "Boris" saw him too, stole the pieces and took them to his turret room where Ivor found them.

First published in 2002 by Usborne Publishing Ltd., Usborne House, 83-85 Saffron Hill, London EC1N 8RT, England. www.usborne.com